DATE DUE

Nuclear Energy

Other Books in the Current Controversies Series

Nuclear Energy

Debra A. Miller, Book Editor

GREENHAVEN PRESS
A part of Gale, Cengage Learning

GALE
CENGAGE Learning™

Detroit • New York • San Francisco • New Haven, Conn • Waterville, Maine • London

8/10

#501404182

GALE
CENGAGE Learning·

Christine Nasso, *Publisher*
Elizabeth Des Chenes, *Managing Editor*

© 2010 Greenhaven Press, a part of Gale, Cengage Learning

Gale and Greenhaven Press are registered trademarks used herein under license.

For more information, contact:
Greenhaven Press
27500 Drake Rd.
Farmington Hills, MI 48331-3535
Or you can visit our Internet site at gale.cengage.com

For product information and technology assistance, contact us at

Gale Customer Support, 1-800-877-4253
For permission to use material from this text or product, submit all requests online at
www.cengage.com/permissions

Further permissions questions can be emailed to permissionrequest@cengage.com

Articles in Greenhaven Press anthologies are often edited for length to meet page require-ments. In addition, original titles of these works are changed to clearly present the main thesis and to explicitly indicate the author's opinion. Every effort is made to ensure that Greenhaven Press accurately reflects the original intent of the authors. Every effort has been made to trace the owners of copyrighted material.

Cover image copyright Nobor, 2010. Used under license from Shutterstock.com.

LIBRARY OF CONGRESS CATALOGING-IN-PUBLICATION DATA

Nuclear energy / Debra A. Miller, book editor.
   p. cm. -- (Current controversies)
   Includes bibliographical references and index.
   ISBN 978-0-7377-4917-5 (hardcover) -- ISBN 978-0-7377-4918-2 (pbk.)
   1. Nuclear industry--Juvenile literature. 2. Nuclear energy--Juvenile literature. 3. Environmental economics--Juvenile literature. I. I. Miller, Debra A.
   HD9698.A2N778 2010
   333.792'4--dc22
                                                   2010001530

Printed in the United States of America
1 2 3 4 5 6 7 14 13 12 11 10

Contents

The nuclear power industry has been extremely successful at avoiding major accidents at nuclear reactor sites. During twelve thousand reactor-years of commercial operation in thirty-two countries, there have been only two major accidents—Three Mile Island and Chernobyl. Neither of these accidents caused large numbers of deaths, and the nuclear industry has since adopted more safety measures.

The accident at the Three Mile Island nuclear plant in Pennsylvania stopped the growth of nuclear power in America for thirty years, but the approach of climate change requires that this energy source be reconsidered. Nuclear power is the only developed energy technology that can safely produce large amounts of electricity without releasing greenhouse gas emissions.

No: Nuclear Energy Is Not a Good Solution to Climate Change

No new nuclear power plants have been built in the United States since the Three Mile Island accident thirty years ago, but today, because of the public concern about global warming, the nuclear industry is poised for a comeback. Several companies have taken steps to build up to eight new generation nuclear plants by 2020, and if this initial wave goes well, other nuclear projects could follow.

Foreword

By definition, controversies are "discussions of questions in which opposing opinions clash" (Webster's Twentieth Century Dictionary Unabridged). Few would deny that controversies are a pervasive part of the human condition and exist on virtually every level of human enterprise. Controversies transpire between individuals and among groups, within nations and between nations. Controversies supply the grist necessary for progress by providing challenges and challengers to the status quo. They also create atmospheres where strife and warfare can flourish. A world without controversies would be a peaceful world; but it also would be, by and large, static and prosaic.

The Series' Purpose

The purpose of the Current Controversies series is to explore many of the social, political, and economic controversies dominating the national and international scenes today. Titles selected for inclusion in the series are highly focused and specific. For example, from the larger category of criminal justice, Current Controversies deals with specific topics such as police brutality, gun control, white collar crime, and others. The debates in Current Controversies also are presented in a useful, timeless fashion. Articles and book excerpts included in each title are selected if they contribute valuable, long-range ideas to the overall debate. And wherever possible, current information is enhanced with historical documents and other relevant materials. Thus, while individual titles are current in focus, every effort is made to ensure that they will not become quickly outdated. Books in the Current Controversies series will remain important resources for librarians, teachers, and students for many years.

In addition to keeping the titles focused and specific, great care is taken in the editorial format of each book in the series. Book introductions and chapter prefaces are offered to provide background material for readers. Chapters are organized around several key questions that are answered with diverse opinions representing all points on the political spectrum. Materials in each chapter include opinions in which authors clearly disagree as well as alternative opinions in which authors may agree on a broader issue but disagree on the possible solutions. In this way, the content of each volume in Current Controversies mirrors the mosaic of opinions encountered in society. Readers will quickly realize that there are many viable answers to these complex issues. By questioning each author's conclusions, students and casual readers can begin to develop the critical thinking skills so important to evaluating opinionated material.

Current Controversies is also ideal for controlled research. Each anthology in the series is composed of primary sources taken from a wide gamut of informational categories including periodicals, newspapers, books, U.S. and foreign government documents, and the publications of private and public organizations. Readers will find factual support for reports, debates, and research papers covering all areas of important issues. In addition, an annotated table of contents, an index, a book and periodical bibliography, and a list of organizations to contact are included in each book to expedite further research.

Perhaps more than ever before in history, people are confronted with diverse and contradictory information. During the Persian Gulf War, for example, the public was not only treated to minute-to-minute coverage of the war, it was also inundated with critiques of the coverage and countless analyses of the factors motivating U.S. involvement. Being able to sort through the plethora of opinions accompanying today's major issues, and to draw one's own conclusions, can be a complicated and frustrating struggle. It is the editors' hope that Current Controversies will help readers with this struggle.

Introduction

"*Nuclear energy research initially was concentrated on producing an atomic bomb for use in World War II. The development of nuclear energy for ... the generation of electricity began only after the war ended in 1945.*"

Nuclear energy is obtained from splitting apart atoms, the basic building block of matter, in a process known as fission. When the atoms split, they release large amounts of energy, which is used to heat water and create steam that, in turn, can be used to spin steam turbines and create electricity. Scientists have known since the turn of the twentieth century that atoms contain massive amounts of energy, and German scientist Albert Einstein published the mathematical formula for the relationship between mass and energy ($E=mc^2$) in 1905. However, scientific theory was not turned into the reality of a sustainable nuclear fission reaction until decades later. Even then, nuclear energy research initially was concentrated on producing an atomic bomb for use in World War II. The development of nuclear energy for civilian purposes such as the generation of electricity began only after the war ended in 1945.

Research into the nature of the atom first began in the late 1800s, a period during which famous French physicist and chemist Marie Curie pioneered the field of radioactivity. Later, in the 1930s, a number of scientists experimented with ways to split the atom. The first person to produce a fission reaction was Italian-American physicist Enrico Fermi in 1934. Fermi successfully split a uranium atom with neutrons (electrically neutral subatomic particles). Later experiments by German and Austrian scientists repeated Fermi's successful atom split, showing that the leftover materials had only half the atomic mass of the original uranium, thereby proving that a fission reaction—that is, the splitting of the uranium atom— had occurred and had released some of the energy of the uranium. This confirmed Einstein's theory that mass is equivalent to the amount of energy held inside atoms.

Scientists around the world next began to explore whether they could produce a sustainable nuclear fission reaction that could produce much larger amounts of energy. A group of scientists led by Fermi, working in the United States at the University of Chicago, constructed the world's first nuclear reactor on the floor of a squash court beneath the school's athletic stadium. Fermi's model nuclear reactor consisted of uranium placed in a stack of graphite together with rods made of cadmium, a material that absorbs neutrons. The purpose of the cadmium rods was to slow the nuclear reaction in order to cause a chain reaction that could be controlled. On December 2, 1942, Fermi and his associates tested the device, producing the world's first self-sustaining nuclear fission reaction—a success that marked the beginning of the nuclear energy age.

Many scientists saw the potential of nuclear energy for both civilian power and for military weapons. Germany's aggressive military movements in Europe and the start of World War II, however, soon directed most nuclear research toward military objectives. Although the Soviet Union also pursued nuclear weapons research, British scientists were among the first to realize the potential of nuclear fission for making powerful atomic bombs. A group of eminent British scientists known as the MAUD Committee concluded in 1941 that a nuclear bomb was feasible, that it would be much more powerful than conventional bombs, and that it would likely release large quantities of dangerous radioactive substances near the explosion site. Because Nazi scientists were also believed to be working on an atomic bomb, Britain pursued the bomb project urgently and sought the cooperation of the United States, hoping to engage additional resources. The Japanese attack on Pearl Harbor in 1941 soon assured U.S. participation.

In 1942, the United States initiated a secret research project—code-named the Manhattan Project and directed by American physicist J. Robert Oppenheimer—which brought together scientists from the United States, Britain, Denmark, and Canada for the purpose of developing the first atomic bomb. The Manhattan Project lasted until 1946, cost about $2 billion, and resulted in two atomic bombs that the United States and its allies used against Japan, the last standing Axis enemy following Germany's surrender in the spring of 1944. The first atomic bomb was made from uranium and was dropped on Hiroshima, Japan, on August 6, 1945. The second bomb, containing plutonium, was dropped on Nagasaki, Japan, on August 9, 1945. Both bombs caused enormous human casualties and property damage as well as long-lasting radiation poisoning. On August 11, 1945, the Japanese government surrendered, and the war officially ended when Japanese officials signed surrender documents on September 2, 1945.

After the war, although nuclear weapons research continued in both the United States and the Soviet Union, the research used to develop nuclear weapons was tapped to develop nuclear reactors that could produce electricity for civilian and commercial use. The first U.S. nuclear reactor was built with government help in Idaho and generated the first nuclear-produced electricity in December 1951. In 1953, U.S. president Dwight Eisenhower proposed an Atoms for Peace program, designed to direct federal monies toward nuclear power development for electricity generation. Private industry soon became involved, causing the U.S. nuclear power industry to grow rapidly during the 1960s. By the 1970s, the United States had more nuclear power plants than any other country in the world, and nuclear energy supplied close to 20 percent of the electricity produced in the country. Nuclear energy was promoted as cheap, environmentally clean, and safe.

In the 1970s and 1980s, however, the safety of nuclear power plants became the subject of public and government scrutiny following two nuclear plant accidents. The first accident involved the meltdown of a nuclear power plant at Three Mile Island near Harrisburg, Pennsylvania. The accident began on March 29, 1979, when large amounts of reactor coolant escaped, and was compounded by human failure in understanding the nature of the problem. Ultimately, the reactor was brought under control and authorities concluded that releases of radiation from the accident had no significant health effects on local residents. Nevertheless, the accident caused widespread public fears about nuclear energy and is credited with stopping nuclear plant construction in the United States. Another more serious accident occurred at the Chernobyl nuclear power plant in the Soviet Union on April 26, 1986. The Chernobyl event began when one of the plant's reactors completely exploded, releasing a plume of highly radioactive fallout over a huge geographical area in the Soviet Union and Europe. Large sections of the Soviet Union were badly contaminated and more than three hundred thousand people were resettled. According to later reports by international organizations, the accident also caused fifty-six deaths and many cases of thyroid cancer. Ultimately, however, both nuclear accidents helped to improve the safety of nuclear power.

Today, with fears about global warming highlighting the need for non–fossil fuel energy sources that do not produce greenhouse gas emissions, many commentators predict a renaissance of nuclear power. Some countries, such as France, already have embraced nuclear power as the main source for electricity production, while other countries, such as China, are actively building nuclear plants to provide electricity in the future. In the United States, significant opposition to nuclear power still exists, and the nuclear industry is struggling to simply replace old plants. This debate about nuclear power is the subject of the viewpoints contained in *Current Controversies: Nuclear Energy.* The authors present a range of views about whether the advantages of nuclear energy outweigh the disadvantages, whether it is safe for humans and the environment, whether it is a good solution to climate change, and what its future role will or should be.

CHAPTER 1

Do the Benefits of Nuclear Power Outweigh the Risks?

Chapter Preface

Nuclear power plants are similar to power plants fueled by fossil fuels with one important difference—the source of power in nuclear plants is a nuclear fission reaction. Fission is basically a process of splitting atoms that releases enormous amounts of heat energy. This heat, in turn, is used to produce steam to drive turbines that generate electricity. The electricity is then fed into the electrical grid and used by homeowners and industry.

Only certain types of material contain atoms that are capable of fission. Uranium—a common radioactive element found in low concentrations in soil, rock, and water—is the only type of fissionable material that occurs naturally in the environment. It undergoes a very slow, spontaneous fission process naturally and constantly emits a low level of radiation from this process, making it the logical choice of fuel for nuclear fission reactors. Most of the earth's uranium resources are made of uranium-238, a type of material that is more difficult to use for fission, while the more easily fissionable uranium-235 is present in only about 0.7 percent of naturally occurring uranium. Uranium-238, however, can be used to produce another type of fissionable material—plutonium-239. Uranium-235 and plutonium-239 are the two main types of fuel used in nuclear power plants.

The nuclear reactor in a nuclear power plant works by shooting neutrons—electrically charged subatomic particles—at a core made of nuclear fuel. When the atoms in the nuclear fuel split, they release a huge amount of heat and radiation. It takes only a small amount of fuel to produce a great deal of heat energy. In fact, just a pound of uranium enriched with uranium-235 is equal to about a million gallons of gasoline. For the reactor core to heat up and continue to produce heat, it must reach a state called critical mass, in which neutrons created by the fission reaction strike other nearby atoms and produce a chain reaction. To reach critical mass, a minimum amount of fuel is needed—two pounds (0.9 kg) of uranium-235 or ten ounces (283 grams) of plutonium-239. In today's light water reactors, this fuel is made into rods and placed together into bundles, and the bundles are submerged in water inside a pressurized tank. The water acts as a coolant, helping to keep the fuel from overheating, and produces steam for the production of electricity.

To keep the nuclear core of fuel at critical mass and control the rate of the nuclear reaction, operators of nuclear plants use control rods made from cadmium, hafnium, or boron—materials that absorb neutrons. By inserting the cadmium rods and decreasing the number of neutrons, the fission reaction can be slowed, reducing the amount of heat generated. Conversely, the rods can be removed to speed up the reaction and produce more heat. The rods can also be used to completely shut down the reactor in the case of an accident or to place fresh fuel in the core. About one-quarter of the fuel rods in a reactor must be replaced every one to two years to keep the plant operating.

One of the main concerns with nuclear fission is the fact that it produces high amounts of radiation—invisible particles that can penetrate many types of matter and cause significant harm and even death to human bodies. Only very dense materials, such as concrete and lead, can stop radioactive particles. To prevent the escape of these radioactive particles into the atmosphere, therefore, nuclear plants typically are massive structures built from concrete and made strong enough to survive earthquakes or crashing planes. Inside these thick concrete exterior walls, the reactor core and equipment are housed within a large steel containment vessel that acts as another barrier to prevent leakage of radioactive gases or fluids. Inside the steel vessel, the core itself is further sealed by another concrete liner, which acts as the first line of defense against the release of radiation. The core is also protected by water and thick lead walls.

Another problem associated with nuclear reactors is the disposal of radioactive nuclear wastes. After fissioning, the spent fuel rods are more radioactive than any material on Earth. Any humans exposed to these wastes would be certain to die from the exposure. Each nuclear power plant produces about twenty metric tons of spent fuel each year, and the amount of highly radioactive fuel produced annually in the United States is roughly two thousand metric tons. About fifty-five thousand metric tons of nuclear waste have already been produced in the United States. This waste eventually will decay to safe levels of radioactivity, but this process takes tens of thousands of years. Nuclear plants deal with radioactive wastes today by cooling it for years and then mixing it with glass and storing it in cooled, concrete structures housed at the plant sites. Efforts have been made to develop nuclear waste dumps in remote locations where wastes could be stored deep underground, but so far these efforts have not been developed due to costs and political opposition.

It is possible to reprocess the spent fuel rods to reuse the fuel. To do this, the spent fuel rods are broken open and the plutonium and uranium are separated from other less radioactive wastes for use in making nuclear weapons or as fuel for breeder reactors, which are more efficient users of uranium than regular reactors. However, critics argue that reprocessing is expensive and does not eliminate all of the radioactive waste product. Even worse, reprocessing produces plutonium in a powder form that is not highly radioactive and easily transportable. In 1976, U.S. president Gerald Ford suspended reprocessing of plutonium in the United States because of concerns that the reprocessed fuel might be stolen or otherwise diverted into nuclear weapons. U.S. president Jimmy Carter made the ban permanent in 1977. U.S. president Ronald

Reagan lifted the ban in 1981, but failed to provide federal funding necessary to restart expensive reprocessing operations.

Nuclear fission energy, therefore, has both negatives and positives. As of July 2008, more than 430 nuclear power plants were in operation around the world, providing about 15 percent of global electricity needs. The United States is home to 104 nuclear power plants that provide about 20 percent of the nation's electricity. Yet, because of concerns about safety, many people view nuclear energy with fear and trepidation. The authors of the viewpoints in this chapter point out the successes and failures of the world's usage of nuclear power.

Nuclear Power Has Many Advantages and Few Risks

Bernard L. Cohen

Bernard L. Cohen is an author and a professor emeritus of physics and astronomy and of environmental and occupational health at the University of Pittsburgh in Pennsylvania.

I must begin with an apology for the fact that this paper is written from the standpoint of an American citizen. All of my research has been based on the United States as a "laboratory," using U.S. statistics and U.S. experience and practices. Hopefully, much of it is applicable to other countries....

Avoiding the Environmental Problems of Fossil Fuels

One important advantage of nuclear power is that it avoids the wide variety of environmental problems arising from burning fossil fuels—coal, oil, and gas. These environmental problems probably exceed those of any other human activity. The ones that have received the most publicity have been "global warming," which is changing the earth's climate; acid rain, which is destroying forests and killing fish; air pollution, which is killing tens of thousands of Americans every year, while degrading our quality of life in many ways; the destructive effects of massive mining for coal; and oil spills, which do great harm to ecological systems....

Global warming: Burning fossil fuels produces vast quantities of carbon dioxide, for example 3.7 tons for each ton of coal burned, and carbon dioxide in the atmosphere traps heat, increasing the earth's temperature. Estimates of the rate of the temperature rise and of the consequences vary, but eventually

Bernard L. Cohen, "The Nuclear Power Advantage," Environmentalists for Nuclear Energy, accessed October 22, 2009. www.ecolo.org/documents/documents_in_english/nuclear_advantage_Cohen.en.htm. Reproduced by permission of the author.

the effects are bound to be important. Agriculture is very sensitive to climate and hence will be heavily affected, requiring shifts in crops that cannot be grown in different areas. Livestock will be affected through problems in breeding, diseases, and pest control. Forests will come under heavy stress as growing areas for each tree species shift and insect populations, disease patterns, competition from other plants, and factors affecting fires change. Eventually, the melting glaciers will cause sea levels to rise—this floods valuable land, escalates the frequency and severity of disasters from hurricanes, allows inland penetration of salt water that heavily impacts aquatic life (e.g., oyster harvests), and leads to loss of urban water supplies and contamination of groundwater. Effects of changing storm tracks, rainfall, and wind patterns are bound to be important.

Nuclear power . . . avoids the wide variety of environmental problems arising from burning fossil fuels—coal, oil, and gas.

The global warming issue has been the subject of a series of high-level international conferences, culminating in a still unratified agreement to reduce carbon dioxide emissions, the implementation of which is estimated to cost the U.S. economy hundreds of billions of dollars per year.

Acid rain: Burning fossil fuels releases large quantities of sulphur dioxide and nitrogen oxide gasses that combine with moisture in the air to produce acids that fall with rain. The effects are complicated and conclusions about them are controversial, but there is strong evidence that, in some cases, acid rain is making lakes unlivable for fish and is badly damaging forests.

Some of the most important problems caused by acid rain are political. The emissions from coal-burning power plants in midwestern United States are the cause of acid rain in eastern

Canada and this has been a top-priority political issue in Canada, making it an important source of difficulty in U.S.-Canadian relations. The situation is similar in Europe where coal-burning emissions from Britain are damaging lakes and forests in Scandinavia and Germany. . . .

Air pollution: While global warming causes only economic disruption, and acid rain kills only fish and trees, air pollution kills people and causes human suffering through illness. Vast amounts of research have gone into understanding the processes involved and tying down the responsible components, but successes have been limited. There are well-recognised health effects from many of the components, sulphur dioxide, nitrogen oxides, carbon monoxide, fine particulates, hydrocarbons, ozone, volatile organic compounds, and toxic metals, but probably the health effects result from combinations of several of these. The problem is complicated by the fact that effects build up slowly over many years or decades, causing illness and weakening constitutions to the point where death eventually results [from] but is not obviously tied to air pollution. The epidemiological evidence, however, seems fairly clear in indicating that something like 30,000 deaths per year in the United States result from air pollution due to emissions from fossil fuel–burning power plants. Shifting from fossil fuel to nuclear power would avert these deaths, and if electricity becomes much more widely used for transportation (e.g., with electric cars), the life saving would be much larger. Human discomfort and ill health are an important part of the price we pay for burning fossil fuels. Economic losses from worker absence and/or reduced efficiency due to illness are also substantial.

Air pollution discolours and otherwise damages buildings, soils clothing, and makes for a generally dirty environment, which adversely impacts on our quality of life.

Coal mining: Sixty percent of U.S. coal is obtained by strip mining, which involves removing up to 200 feet of covering soil. There are laws and good-faith efforts to reclaim the land, but these have had only limited success, and the land is often left badly scarred. The remaining 40 percent of coal comes from underground mines, and this percentage is increasing. Acid drainage from these mines gets into streams, killing fish and leaving the water unfit for drinking, swimming, or many industrial applications. About one-fourth of the 8 million acres of U.S. land about coal mines has subsided causing buildings on the surface to crack or even be destroyed, and often changing drainage patterns so as to make land unfit for farming. There are hundreds of long-lasting fires in U.S. mines that release air polluting smoke and vegetation-destroying heat, often for many years. Waste banks from coal washing outside mines are unsightly and frequently catch fire, leading to another source of air pollution.

Oil spills: The highly publicised 40,000 ton oil spill off the coast of Alaska in 1989, even after 10 years of cleanup costing several billion dollars, has still left substantial long-term damage to the ecology of the region. But there have been much larger oil spills, including one of 305,000 tons off the coast of Tobago [one of the islands that make up the Republic of Trinidad and Tobago] in 1979 and one of 237,000 tons, which ruined many miles of French beaches in 1978. U.S. tankers spill several hundred thousand tons of oil each year on average. At any given time, 100 million tons of oils are transported by ships, so accidental spills are inevitable. Land-based accidents can also be important. A Mexican well that could not be capped spilled 700,000 tons of oil into the Gulf of Mexico in 1979, doing extensive damage to the aquatic life. . . .

Fuel Resources

Another nuclear advantage is in the nature of the fuel consumed. Oil and gas are the principal fuels used for space heating and for transportation and are difficult to replace in those applications. The world's supply of these is limited, probably enough for less than 100 years of projected consumption, and costs are bound to rise sharply long before supplies are exhausted. Coal can be used to produce further supplies of oil and gas, but its supply is also limited. Coal, oil and gas are the principal feedstocks for producing plastics and organic chemicals, without which our technological society would be severely crippled. There is thus every reason to preserve our supplies of fossil fuels. Uranium for nuclear fuel, on the other hand, has little value for other purposes, and with breeder reactors, there is enough to satisfy world energy needs for billions of years, without increasing the cost of electricity by as much as one percent.

Uranium for nuclear fuel ... has little value for other purposes, and with breeder reactors, there is enough to satisfy world energy needs for billions of years.

Waste Disposal Issues

We have been bombarded with propaganda about the potential dangers of long-lived radioactive waste from nuclear reactors. But these wastes have the extremely important advantage of being very small in volume and can be easily contained so they can be buried deep underground. The results of an analysis ... indicate that the wastes from coal burning, including those that end up in the ground, are far more dangerous. These include chemical carcinogens like beryllium, cadmium, arsenic, nickel, and chromium, which unlike the nuclear wastes, last forever. They also include uranium, which occurs as an impurity in coal, ends up in the top surfaces of the ground, and serves as a source for random emissions; nuclear power, in contrast, consumes uranium, thus averting future deaths from exposure to radon gas. . . .

Nuclear Bombs

Much has been made of the connection between nuclear power and nuclear bombs, although the relationship is really very weak. There are much easier, faster, and cheaper ways for nations to develop nuclear weapons than through a nuclear power programme. All nuclear weapon states have developed their bombs independently from their electricity generation facilities, and any nation with a serious desire to obtain nuclear weapons could and would do the same. The problem here is not so much to avoid the development of nuclear bombs that is essentially a lost cause as to avoid their use. One of the most likely scenarios for their use is in fighting over oil as world supplies dwindle to precarious levels during the twenty-first century. Oil resources are limited and located largely in the politically unstable Middle East, so that competition for it can become intense. The 1991 Persian Gulf War could easily be a forerunner of much more serious confrontations. However, electricity can replace oil for space heating and produce hydrogen as a substitute for oil in transportation applications. Nuclear power thus has the advantage of mitigating the need for oil, thereby avoiding one of the prime potential reasons for using nuclear bombs.

[Nuclear] wastes [are] ... very small in volume and can be easily contained so they can be buried deep underground.

Accident Risks

The public has been bombarded with fears of reactor accidents, nearly always focussing on the effects of the worst accident evaluated in some study, and never treating the probability of such an accident. In fact, it is often said that probability doesn't matter; the only important thing is the worst possible accident. To face the accident risk squarely, one must recognise that it is absolutely essential for probability to be considered because there is no such thing as the worst possible accident—any hypothetical accident can be made worse by extenuating circumstances, albeit with reduced probability.

The risk to an average American of a very large nuclear power program in the United States is equivalent to the risk of a regular smoker smoking one extra cigarette every 15 years.

For example, one of the innumerable gasoline tank trucks that roam our streets can have a collision spilling the fuel, leading to a fire that could destroy a whole city, killing millions of people. It might require a lot of improbable circumstances combining together, like water lines being frozen to prevent effective firefighting, a traffic jam aggravated by road construction or other accidents limiting access to firefighters, substandard gas pipes that the heat of the fire causes to leak, a high wind frequently shifting to spread the fire in all directions, a strong atmospheric temperature inversion after the whole city becomes engulfed in flames that keeps the smoke close to the ground, bridges and tunnels closed for various reasons to eliminate escape routes, errors in advising the public, and so forth. Each of these situations is improbable, so a combination of many of them occurring in sequence is highly improbable, but not impossible. If anyone thinks that is the worst possible accident, consider the possibility of the fire being spread by glowing embers to other cities that were left without protection because their firefighters were off assisting the first city, etc.

As an example for nuclear's chief competitor, coal burning, consider the possibility of the abundant mutagenic chemicals it produces leading to the development of a virus that could wipe out mankind; a virus as deadly as HIV that could be as easily spread as the influenza virus could come close to that! There is no such thing as the worst possible accident, and probability must be considered.

This is another important advantage for nuclear power—the probabilities have been determined and they are very small indeed. The best way to display this advantage is to compare the risks of nuclear power with other risks. . . .

This advantage can perhaps be expressed more clearly by saying the risk to an average American of a very large nuclear power program in the United States is equivalent to the risk of a regular smoker smoking one extra cigarette every 15 years, or to the risk of an overweight person increasing his weight by 0.012 ounces, or of raising the U.S. highway speed limit from 55 to 55.006 miles per hour.

Nuclear power [thus] has advantages in many areas, including some that have been traditionally viewed as problem areas. It averts the pollution and environmental degradation of fossil fuels; it guarantees the world an everlasting supply of fuel without affecting resources sorely needed for other applications; it solves difficult waste management problems; it contributes to avoidance of nuclear warfare, and it diminishes risks from accidents.

Nuclear Energy Gains Bipartisan Support as Global Warming Worsens

Patrick Moore

Patrick Moore is an environmental activist and is cochair of the Clean and Safe Energy Coalition.

A new, bipartisan consensus is building around the environmental benefits of nuclear energy in America.

Just a few weeks ago [September 2009], in a meadow in Rocky Mountain National Park, Democratic Sen. Mark Udall of Colorado joined Republican Sen. John McCain of Arizona in concluding that nuclear energy "has to be part of the solution" as the country seeks to reduce its carbon footprint and help reduce greenhouse gas emissions.

The debate about nuclear energy in Oregon, and across much of America, has been a highly emotional, often partisan affair. This new alliance is a breath of fresh air, representing a fundamental shift in political alignment. Fifty-nine percent of Americans polled by Gallup earlier this year said they support nuclear energy as one way to meet the nation's electricity needs.

For more than a decade, Oregon has chosen to remain on the sidelines of the issue. Now may be the right time for this state to consider putting nuclear energy back to work on behalf of clean air and economic growth.

The Value of Nuclear Energy

I understand Oregon's reservations. I once had them, too. But after four decades as an active environmentalist, studying the facts, my views have evolved—and I'm not alone.

Patrick Moore, "A Changing Climate Around Nuclear Energy," *Statesman Journal*, October 12, 2009. www.statesmanjournal.com. Reproduced by permission of the author.

Several leaders and groups within the environmental movement now recognize that the nuclear energy industry has a stellar safety record and can meet the nation's rising electricity demand with virtually emissions-free energy. Nuclear energy is one of the best clean energy options to deliver the power we need without producing air pollution and greenhouse gases.

The nuclear energy industry has a stellar safety record and can meet the nation's rising electricity demand with virtually emissions-free energy.

Along with hydroelectric power, nuclear energy is the only non-emitting baseload energy source operating around the clock, providing one-fifth of the energy powering U.S. homes and businesses. And nuclear energy already produces 72 percent of all carbon-free electricity in the country.

Just to the south, California's four nuclear reactors prevent millions of tons of CO_2 from entering the atmosphere, emissions that would otherwise be generated by natural gas power plants or out-of-state coal generating facilities.

According to recent polls, for the first time in three decades a majority of Californians support nuclear energy. And earlier this month, Sen. Barbara Boxer, D-Calif., announced the Senate's climate change legislation will include support for nuclear energy.

Like Oregon, California has set aggressive targets for emissions reductions over the coming decades, and nuclear energy can go a long way to help meet them. Others, including Florida and Ohio, have formally recognized this by introducing legislation allowing nuclear energy to be included in a range of technologies to meet clean or alternative energy standards.

A Source of Economic Growth

Nuclear energy's growing appeal is also based on economics. In Oregon, where the jobless rate has nearly doubled in the past 12 months, the thousands of construction jobs that a new nuclear reactor brings would be welcome. And the 400–700 high-paying permanent positions added to operate each plant would bring opportunity to workers who deserve a chance to build a stable career in their communities.

Oregon State continues to be a leader in the development of advanced nuclear energy plant designs. Researchers there helped develop many of the new safety systems that have been incorporated in the designs of the 25 new reactors in the federal government permitting process. And it is working on a five-year, $6 million grant to help engineer future reactors.

Taken together, it's no wonder that political leaders of all stripes, business advocates and an increasing number of environmentalists are looking at nuclear energy as a source for economic growth, energy security and cleaner air. It's no longer a question of whether, but when Oregon should be part of the discussion on how to deploy nuclear energy.

Nuclear Energy Is an Integral Part of a Practical Climate Change Solution

David Kalson

David Kalson is a writer and communications consultant with expertise in a number of areas, including energy, science, and technology.

"Facts are stubborn things," said Jacques Besnainou, CEO of AREVA NC [a nuclear power company]. Invoking John Adams's quote, he was not referring to just any facts, but to facts about nuclear power, particularly as it applies to the U.S., at the Tuck Speaker Series of the French-American Foundation, held in New York on June 8th [2009]. And the stubbornness of his facts is likely problematic to nuclear power opponents. How do they argue against reliable, proven, non-CO_2-emitting power, jobs and the long-term regional economic development that Besnainou maintains nuclear power promises the U.S.?

Proliferation? Waste? These are emotional issues rather than insurmountable technical hurdles, Besnainou believes, but he's certainly open to engaging in the debate. Cost? A solvable political problem that he's optimistic will be addressed by Congress.

The night's discussion between Besnainou and Dr. Charles Ferguson, a physicist and senior fellow for science and technology at the Council on Foreign Relations [CFR, a U.S. research center], mostly centered on Besnainou's "stubborn things," including his conclusion: "Nuclear power," he said, "is not the solution (to our energy challenges), but there is no solution without nuclear power."

David Kalson, "Stubborn Facts About Nuclear Power," The Energy Collective, July 1, 2009. http://theenergycollective.com. Reproduced by permission of the author.

Nuclear Power Needed to Fight Climate Change

True, similar statements are often made about coal and could also be made about efficiency or renewables. But, this seeming surfeit of partial solutions only drives home a point on which most scientists, and at least some policy makers, readily agree: To stave off global climate change and power ourselves through the mid-21st century, we need every non-CO_2 or, at least, reduced-CO_2, source of energy we can get our hands on—along with every conceivable efficiency measure.

Nuclear power must take its rightfully earned place, Besnainou said, among efficiency, smart grids, renewables, "clean" coal, etc. But he made an important distinction. Unlike some of our energy options for fighting climate change, such as "clean" coal and smart grids, technologies that are likely to be decades off in the future, nuclear power technology is here now.

Unlike [climate change] technologies that are likely to be decades off in the future, nuclear power technology is here now.

And, as a baseload energy source, nuclear power complements peaking sources, such as wind. "To me," he said, "it's nonsense to be pro wind power and against nuclear."

Emotional Concerns About Nuclear Power

Besnainou backs his views about nuclear power's necessary role in our energy futures with formidable personal credentials (he holds degrees in math and engineering) and a company with a successful nuclear track record. AREVA has built 100 nuclear plants around the world and is the number one supplier of nuclear energy products/services in North America with $2.5 billion in North American sales.

"We've done it for 40 years in France," he said. But he also acknowledged that even with many undeniable scientific truths on its side, nuclear power is as much an emotional matter as it is scientific. And thus he dismissed the usual criticisms of nuclear as more emotionally driven rather than anything worthy of serious scientific concern:

Proliferation: It can be managed, Besnainou said simply. He pointed out, and it was rather persuasive, that the countries representing the biggest threats of nuclear proliferation, North Korea and Iran, have never produced one megawatt of power from nuclear energy.

Terrorist attacks: [They] can be managed as well. Charles Ferguson of CFR agreed that both the proliferation and terror issues were not sufficient to stop this energy source. They are "manageable risks" and were thus rather quickly, indeed, too quickly, dispensed with at this evening's discussion.

Energy security: Nuclear power in the U.S., Besnainou said, represents a quasi-domestic source of energy. Uranium fuel is well distributed in the world, including in stable countries, such as Canada and Australia. Plus, nuclear power will contribute to the electric car's growth, thereby playing a key role in the transportation sector while helping to wean countries off foreign oil.

Cost: Besnainou argued that when *everything* is factored in, including recycling nuclear waste and a price on carbon from traditional plants, and you add in the costs of handling coal waste, nuclear power is entirely competitive with other energy sources.

Recycling: Besnainou listed the reasons why nuclear fuel recycling was beneficial and, again, he was persuasive, deeming nuclear power a cradle-to-cradle energy solution, where 96 percent of used nuclear fuel is recyclable. Recycled nuclear waste also is reduced to one-fifth its original volume and one-tenth its toxicity.

In closing, Dr. Ferguson asked if Besnainou felt that the U.S. should emulate the French nuclear model, where nuclear power represents 80 percent of French generation. Besnainou pointed out that for the U.S. to simply maintain its current proportion of nuclear power, now at 20 percent, the U.S. would need to build 35 new reactors.

Nuclear power [is] a cradle-to-cradle energy solution, where 96 percent of used nuclear fuel is recyclable.

Ferguson asked how the U.S. establishment could pressure Congress to act on behalf of nuclear. Besnainou answered, "In Congress we need a strong bipartisan coalition, and it's coming." He clearly believes that stubborn facts will prevail in the face of emotionalism.

Nuclear Energy Disasters Are Inevitable

Rose Kivi

Rose Kivi is a writer from Los Angeles who enjoys writing on a variety of topics.

If the history of nuclear power plant disasters can teach us anything, it can teach us that nuclear power plant accidents can never be one hundred percent avoidable. This article ... details some of the worst nuclear power plant accidents in history.

Nuclear Power Plant Disasters

Accidents in nuclear power plants happen for a variety of reasons, most commonly they are a result of human errors and faulty equipment. Even power plants that provide the strictest of safety measures cannot be considered one hundred percent foolproof. Safety measures do not account for the unforeseen or for human error.

Nuclear power plant disasters have contaminated humans, animals and the environment. It is not possible to fully know all of the harmful effects that resulted from these disasters since radiation exposure to humans, animals and the environment can have many long-term effects.

Due to the number of health and environmental dangers associated with contamination from nuclear plants, the possibility of future nuclear power plant accidents causing radiation contamination to humans, animals and the environment understandably has made some people very concerned with the operation of current nuclear power plants and the possible construction of new ones in the future.

Rose Kivi, "A History of Nuclear Power Plant Disasters," Bright Hub, July 31, 2009. www.brighthub.com. Reproduced by permission of the author.

Chalk River—December 12, 1952

The accident in the Chalk River facility in Canada was caused by mistakes made by employees. An employee accidentally opened four valves that regulated pressure in the system. The opened valves changed pressure causing control rods to partially come out of the reactor. Safety measures were attempted that led to another mistake of a wrong button being pushed. Power output in the reactor rose and the lid blew off the reactor. Large amounts of cooling water contaminated with radioactive waste leaked into the facility. Crews were brought in to contain and clean up the radioactive materials.

Even [nuclear] power plants that provide the strictest of safety measures cannot be considered one hundred percent foolproof.

Mayak Plutonium Facility—
September 29, 1957

An accident at the Mayak plutonium facility in the South Ural Mountains of Russia is considered by some to have been worse than Chernobyl. Cooling equipment at the Mayak facility broke down and failed to cool nuclear waste. The overheated nuclear waste exploded. Approximately 270,000 people and 14,000 square miles were exposed to radiation. Five hundred square miles were exposed to extremely high levels of radiation. Prior to the 1957 accident, the Mayak facility had a history of contaminating the environment with radioactive material through dumping in nearby water sources and several accidents. The accident in 1957 was the most severe of the incidents with the power plant. Today, radiation levels in the area are among the highest in the world, with natural water sources in the area still contaminated with radioactive waste.

Windscale Nuclear Power Plant— October 10, 1957

An accident occurred at the Windscale nuclear power plant in England that caused a radiation leak that spread 200 square miles. Faulty equipment at the plant gave inaccurate temperature readings. The temperature readings showed that equipment was cooler than it actually was. Employees' actions that resulted from the inaccurate readings caused the reactor to overheat and graphite in the plant to burn. The burning graphite caused a fire that was not fully put out until the next day, when employees released mass amounts of water into the facility to put out the fire and cool off the reactors. Filters installed in the chimneys of the plant prevented some of the radiation from escaping into the environment. But even those precautions could not prevent the widespread contamination that occured.

Filters installed in the chimneys ... could not prevent the widespread contamination that occurred [at the Windscale nuclear power plant].

Lubmin Nuclear Power Plant— December 7, 1975

A fire at the Lubmin nuclear power plant in East Germany caused safety systems to fail. Employees quickly acted to release coolant into the facility and avoided a nuclear meltdown.

Three Mile Island—March 28, 1979

The accident at Three Mile Island in Pennsylvania resulted from a malfunction in the cooling system. The malfunction in the cooling system caused the reactor to shut down. Rising pressure in the reactor caused a relief valve to open. The relief valve was located at the top of the pressurizer. The relief valve opened and poured water into the pressurizer, but did not shut when it was supposed to. Employees at the plant did not realize that the relief valve was open, and responded to the increased pressure in the pressurizer by reducing coolant flow. Without any gauges that measured the core coolant level or the position of the valve, the employees wrongfully assumed that the high water levels in the pressurizer sensed by the gauges meant that the coolant level in the core was too high. When the employees reduced the coolant, the system overheated and destroyed the fuel rods, which leaked radiation into the cooling water. Once employees realized what had happened, they were able to release a flow of emergency water into the system to cool it and prevent further mishap.

Nearby residents to the plant who were pregnant and small children were eventually evacuated from the area for health concerns. To date, there are still numerous studies investigating the increased rates of cancer and thyroid problems associated with the incident on top of the sharp change in the rate of infant mortalities that occurred at the time. The health risks associated with the Three Mile Island incident are still hotly debated but new research is beginning to show the real dangers of radiation contamination.

Chernobyl—April 26, 1986

The accident at the Chernobyl nuclear power plant in the Ukraine [then a part of the Soviet Union] was caused by a faulty reactor design combined with mistakes made by power plant employees. A surge of power destroyed one of the reactors at the plant and released large amounts of radiation. Helicopters dropped boron and sand onto the reactor to prevent more radiation from leaking into the environment.

Six hundred employees were present at the time of the explosion. Of the 600 employees present, 134 were exposed to high levels of radiation. Two employees died within hours. Another 28 employees died within the next four months. Six hundred thousand people who participated in the radiation cleanup were also exposed to radiation. Approximately two hundred thousand of the people who participated in the cleanup were exposed to levels of radiation that are deemed unsafe. The radiation exposure from the plant spread far and exposed approximately 5 million people who lived in the contaminated areas.

The radiation exposure from [the accident at the Chernobyl nuclear power plant] ... spread far and exposed approximately 5 million people who lived in the contaminated areas.

Even though most of the 5 million were only exposed to low levels of radiation, it is impossible to know the amount of health problems that can be blamed on the radiation exposure due to the large number of people exposed and the long-term effects; however some deaths and illnesses have been tracked such as the thyroid cancer in 4,000 exposed children, which has been attributed to the radiation exposure. Of those diagnosed with the painful and life-threatening disease, at least nineteen died early on.

Tokaimura, Japan—September 30, 1999

On September 30, 1999, there was an accident at a nuclear power facility ran by JCO Company in Tokaimura, Japan. The accident was caused as a result of an error made by JCO employees. The accident occurred when JCO employees used too much uranium in the uranium nitric acid mix the plant used to make nuclear fuel. The employees added 35 pounds of uranium to the tank that contained the nitric acid, instead of the 5.2 pounds that they were supposed to use. The improper mix caused a nuclear fission chain reaction explosion to occur. The company brought mass amounts of boron to the plant to absorb the radiation, but could not get near enough to the source to spread the boron. Instead, they broke the water pipes that led to the tank, to flood the area and stop the nuclear reaction. After approximately 20 hours, the nuclear reaction was stopped.

Approximately 39 employees were exposed to measurable levels of radiation as a result of the accident. Three employees were exposed to very high levels of radiation, two of which eventually died as a result of the radiation contamination.

Nuclear Energy Is Costly, Dangerous, and Ineffective

Physicians for Social Responsibility

Physicians for Social Responsibility is a nonprofit organization that advocates for policies to prevent nuclear war and to reverse the harmful effects of global warming on the environment.

The nuclear industry is trying to revitalize itself by manipulating the public's concerns about global warming and energy insecurity to promote nuclear power as a clean and safe way to curb emissions of greenhouse gases and reduce dependence on foreign energy resources. Despite these claims by industry proponents, a thorough examination of the full life cycle of nuclear power generation reveals nuclear power to be a dirty, dangerous and expensive form of energy that poses serious risks to human health, national security and U.S. taxpayers.

Nuclear Power Is Dirty

Each year, enormous quantities of radioactive waste are created during the nuclear fuel process, including 2,000 metric tons of high-level radioactive waste and 12 million cubic feet of low-level radioactive waste in the U.S. alone. About 63,000 metric tons of highly radioactive spent fuel already has accumulated at reactor sites around the U.S. The only proposed permanent repository site, at Yucca Mountain in Nevada, has been cancelled. It could not safely contain the radioactivity and protect the public. Another 42,000 metric tons will be produced by operating reactors. U.S. taxpayers have already paid out $565 million in contract damages to nuclear utilities, because the U.S. government has failed to dispose of the exist-

Physicians for Social Responsibility, "Dirty, Dangerous and Expensive: The Truth About Nuclear Power," 2009. www.psr.org. Reproduced by permission.

ing inventory of spent fuel by the contractual deadline of 1998. An additional billion dollars of damage payments are expected every year for the next decade.

Uranium, which must be removed from the ground, is used to fuel nuclear reactors. Uranium mining, which creates serious health and environmental problems, has disproportionately impacted indigenous people because much of the world's uranium is located under indigenous land. Uranium miners experience higher rates of lung cancer, tuberculosis and other respiratory diseases. The production of 1,000 tons of uranium fuel generates approximately 100,000 tons of radioactive tailings and nearly one million gallons of liquid waste containing heavy metals and arsenic in addition to radioactivity. These uranium tailings have contaminated rivers and lakes. A new method of uranium mining, known as in-situ leaching, does not produce tailings but it does threaten contamination of groundwater supplies.

Serious Safety Concerns

Despite proponents' claims that it is safe, the history of nuclear energy is marked by a number of disasters and near disasters. The 1986 Chernobyl disaster in Ukraine is one of the most horrific examples of the potentially catastrophic consequences of a nuclear accident. An estimated 220,000 people were displaced from their homes, and the radioactive fallout from the accident made 4,440 square kilometers of agricultural land and 6,820 square kilometers of forests in Belarus and Ukraine unusable. It is extremely difficult to get accurate information about the health effects from Chernobyl. Government agencies in Ukraine, Russia, and Belarus estimate that about 25,000 of the 600,000 involved in firefighting and cleanup operations have died so far because of radiation exposure from the accident. According to an April 2006 report commissioned by the European Greens for the European Parliament, there will be an additional 30,000 to 60,000 fatal cancer deaths worldwide from the accident.

In 1979, the United States had its own disaster following an accident at the Three Mile Island nuclear reactor in Pennsylvania. Although there were no immediate deaths, the incident had serious health consequences for the surrounding area. A 1997 study found that those people living downwind of the reactor at the time of the event were two to ten times more likely to contract lung cancer or leukemia than those living upwind of the radioactive fallout. The dangers of nuclear power have been underscored more recently by the close call of a catastrophic meltdown at the Davis-Besse reactor in Ohio in 2002, which in the years preceding the incident had received a near perfect safety score.

Despite proponents' claims that it is safe, the history of nuclear energy is marked by a number of disasters and near disasters.

Climate change may further increase the risk of nuclear accidents. Heat waves, which are expected to become more frequent and intense as a result of global warming, can force the shutdown or the power output reduction of reactors. During the 2006 heat wave, reactors in Michigan, Pennsylvania, Illinois, and Minnesota, as well as in France, Spain, and Germany, were impacted. The European heat wave in the summer of 2003 caused cooling problems at French reactors that forced engineers to tell the government that they could no longer guarantee the safety of the country's 58 nuclear power reactors.

Proliferation, Loose Nukes and Terrorism

The inextricable link between nuclear energy and nuclear weapons is arguably the greatest danger of nuclear power. The same process used to manufacture low-enriched uranium for nuclear fuel also can be employed for the production of highly enriched uranium for nuclear weapons. As it has in the past, expansion of nuclear power could lead to an increase in the number of both nuclear weapons states and 'threshold' nuclear states that could quickly produce weapons by utilizing facilities and materials from their 'civil' nuclear programs, a scenario many fear may be playing out in Iran. Expanded use of nuclear power would increase the risk that commercial nuclear technology will be used to construct clandestine weapons facilities, as was done by Pakistan.

The same process used to manufacture low-enriched uranium for nuclear fuel also can be employed for the production of highly enriched uranium for nuclear weapons.

In addition to uranium, plutonium can also be used to make a nuclear bomb. Plutonium, which is found only in extremely small quantities in nature, is produced in nuclear reactors. Reprocessing spent fuel to separate plutonium from the highly radioactive barrier in spent fuel rods, as is being proposed as a 'waste solution' under the Global Nuclear Energy Partnership program, increases the risk that the plutonium can be diverted or stolen for the production of nuclear weapons or radioactive 'dirty' bombs. Reprocessing is also the most polluting part of the nuclear fuel cycle. The reprocessing facility in France, La Hague, is the world's largest anthropogenic source of radioactivity and its releases have been found in the Arctic Circle.

In addition to the threat of nuclear materials, nuclear reactors are themselves potential terrorist targets. Nuclear reactors are not designed to withstand attacks using large aircraft, such as those used on September 11, 2001. A well-coordinated attack could have severe consequences for human health and the environment. A study by the Union of Concerned Scientists [a research group] concluded that a major attack on the Indian Point reactor in Westchester County, New York, could result in 44,000 near-term deaths from acute radiation sickness and more than 500,000 long-term deaths from cancer among individuals within 50 miles of the reactor.

Nuclear Power Doesn't Mean Energy Independence

Assertions that nuclear power can lead us to energy independence are incorrect. In 2007, more than 90 percent of the uranium used in U.S. nuclear power reactors was imported. The U.S. only has the ninth largest reasonably assured uranium resources in the world. Most of it is low to medium grade, which is not only more polluting but also less economical than uranium found in other nations. The U.S.'s high-priced uranium resources and world uranium price volatility mean that current dependence on foreign sources of uranium is not likely to change significantly in the future.

One country that the U.S. continues to rely on for uranium is Russia. The continuing resolution signed into law in September 2008 extended and expanded the program to import Russian highly enriched uranium that has been down-blended for use in U.S. commercial reactors. This program, which was set to expire in 2013, has been extended through 2020 and expanded to allow more uranium imports per year from Russia. While the program is an important non-proliferation measure (highly enriched uranium can be used to make a nuclear weapon), it means that the U.S. will continue to rely on Russia for a significant amount of uranium for commercial nuclear reactors.

Nuclear Is Expensive

In 1954, then chairman of the Atomic Energy Commission Lewis Strauss promised that the nuclear industry would one day provide energy "too cheap to meter." More than 50 years and tens of billions of dollars in federal subsidies later, nuclear power remains prohibitively expensive. Despite the poor economics, the federal government has continued to pour money into the nuclear industry—the Energy Policy Act of 2005 included more than $17 billion in production subsidies and tax breaks, plus loan guarantees and other incentives for nuclear power.

Nuclear power is neither renewable nor clean, and therefore not a wise option.

The most important subsidy for the nuclear industry—and the most expensive for U.S. taxpayers—comes in the form of loan guarantees, which are promises that taxpayers will bail out the nuclear utilities by paying back their loans when the projects fail. There are currently $18.5 billion authorized for nuclear loan guarantees; the nuclear industry is seeking over $100 billion in guarantees. According to the Congressional Budget Office, the failure rate for nuclear projects is "very high—well above 50 percent." Moody's has called new reactors a "bet the farm" investment.

Making the Safe, Sustainable Investment

It is clear that alternatives to fossil fuels must be developed on a large scale. However, nuclear power is neither renewable nor · clean, and therefore not a wise option. Even if one were to disregard the waste problems, safety risks and dismal economics, nuclear power is both too slow and too limited a solution to global warming and energy insecurity. Given the urgent need to begin reducing greenhouse gas emissions, the long lead times required for the design, permitting and construction of nuclear reactors render nuclear power an ineffective option for addressing global warming.

Taxpayer dollars would be better spent on increasing energy conservation, efficiency and developing renewable energy resources. In fact, numerous studies have shown that improving energy efficiency is the most cost-effective and sustainable way to concurrently reduce energy demand and curb greenhouse gas emissions. New reactors will cost two to three times more than renewable and efficiency technologies. Even the price of electricity from photovoltaic power, one of the most expensive renewable technologies, is falling quickly. Conversely, the cost of nuclear power continues to rise.

When the very serious risk of accidents, proliferation, terrorism and nuclear war are considered, it is clear that investment in nuclear power as a climate change solution is not only misguided, but also highly dangerous. As we look for solutions to the dual threats of global warming and energy insecurity, we should focus our efforts on improving energy conservation and efficiency and expanding the use of safe, clean, renewable forms of energy to build a new energy future for the nation.

The Threat of Nuclear Accidents Persists

Rebecca Harms

Rebecca Harms is a member of the European Parliament (MEP)—a governing body of the European Union—representing Germany. She is also a spokesperson of the Green German MEPs, vice president of the Greens/European Free Alliance, and a leading campaigner against nuclear power.

Ever since atom splitting has been used to generate energy, its risks and dangers have been controversial at least.

And since the disastrous accident at the Chernobyl nuclear power plant in 1986, this debate has in reality been settled in Europe: The majority of the continent's citizens are against this technology.

Proponents of nuclear fission have been trying to jump on the climate change bandwagon to resuscitate nuclear power after decades of stagnation. Unfortunately, some UN [United Nations] climate change strategists, as well as parts of the European Commission, have bought into the nuclear lobby's arguments.

Recent Nuclear Incidents

While we clearly need to reform our wasteful and polluting energy industry to meet today's energy and environmental challenges, grasping at even more dangerous straws cannot be the answer.

Even if the Germans, Swedish and Japanese live under the illusion that their own facilities are by comparison the safest, the operators of atomic facilities have often only avoided a repeat of the Chernobyl disaster by a hair's breadth.

Rebecca Harms, "Nuclear: The Risks Remain," *New Statesman*, July 23, 2007. Reproduced by permission.

Only a couple of weeks ago in the end of June [2007], thick clouds of smoke poured out of a transformer in the nuclear power plant in Krümmel, Germany. The statement of operator Vattenfall claiming the fire in the transformer had no effect on the reactor itself proved to be misleading.

The same day the reactor in Brunsbüttel, a Vattenfall reactor as well, had to be shut down due to network problems. Both incidents were assigned the lowest problem classification in the Vattenfall report—"N" for normal.

The operators of atomic facilities have often only avoided a repeat of the Chernobyl disaster by a hair's breadth.

Also in last year's incident in the Swedish Forsmark reactor, Vattenfall tried to gloss over the seriousness of the situation. The Vattenfall policy of downplaying the actual problems, releasing information only bit by bit and even releasing wrong information is irresponsible and leaves one wondering what else they might be hiding.

Only a couple of days after the incidents in Germany the worldwide biggest nuclear power plant Kashiwazaki-Kariwa in Japan made it to the headlines. An earthquake had caused a series of problems, including a fire in a transformer, a leak in a cooling pond and the damaging of a number of barrels containing nuclear waste. Also here the operator delayed communicating the real scale of the problems to the public.

A High-Risk Technology

The incidents have shown that nuclear energy is not the modern high technology sector portrayed by the industry itself. Aging reactors, the disability to prepare for natural disasters and a safety culture that is at least questionable pose a permanent risk to the population.

It is wrong to try and counteract the risk of global warming through an expansion of nuclear energy and the consequential nuclear risks. Promoting nuclear as a sustainable energy source, as the nuclear lobby in Brussels [Belgium] and elsewhere is trying to do, is misleading. Any technology that can produce such devastating consequences as those in 1986 from the Chernobyl disaster can never be sustainable. Nuclear energy is a high-risk technology.

The permanent risk of a core meltdown is a strong argument against the use of nuclear power.

We can lull ourselves into a false sense of security by trying to forget about past catastrophes. However, the fact that there has not been another accident with a core meltdown since Three Mile Island does not mean that it will never happen again. Every year there are thousands of incidents, occurrences and events in nuclear installations and, simply because there was no catastrophic radioactive leakage, the world reacts as if there was no problem.

The permanent risk of a core meltdown is a strong argument against the use of nuclear power. The lifetime extension of nuclear power plants heightens the risk of a major accident considerably. Are we going to find a solution to dispose of nuclear waste safely for thousands or even millions of years? This question does not only still lack an answer, it goes far beyond imagination. Every country using nuclear power could build a nuclear bomb if it decided to do so. These dangers are no less terrifying given the challenges of climate change.

Only a strategy which finally makes energy companies, ministers and citizens abandon the energy production fix will help fight against climate change. Conservation and efficiency must become priorities in energy supply and use worldwide.

Only negawatt instead of megawatt and the swift expansion of renewable energy sources can put the brakes on climate change.

CHAPTER 2

Is Nuclear Energy Safe for Humans and the Environment?

Chapter Preface

The year 2009 marked the thirty-year anniversary of the world's first major nuclear power plant accident at the Three Mile Island (TMI) plant near Harrisburg, Pennsylvania. The March 28, 1979, accident sparked widespread public fear about the safety of nuclear energy and halted the expansion of the nuclear industry in the United States. Not a single new commercial nuclear power plant has been built in the country since the TMI incident. In 1986, another even more serious nuclear accident occurred at the Chernobyl nuclear power plant in Ukraine, then part of the Soviet Union. Although these two events constitute the only major accidents in the entire history of the nuclear industry, many people continue to see them as reminders of the potential dangers of nuclear power.

The accident at TMI in 1979 was caused both by equipment failure and human error on the part of plant operators. A malfunction in a cooling pump caused a loss of cooling water to the reactor's core, causing the core to heat up. Very quickly, however, the plant's automated response system sent control rods into the reactor and shut down the core, stopping the nuclear fission reaction and preventing an explosion. Another malfunction then caused operators to believe, mistakenly, that there was too much pressure in the reactor and they shut down water pumps, allowing coolant levels to drop. Even though the fission process had been stopped, the lack of coolant allowed the uranium core to generate enough heat to cause a partial meltdown of the reactor. Workers at the plant eventually understood what was happening, but by then radioactive steam had built up in auxiliary tanks, so plant operators directed the steam to waste tanks. During this process some of the steam leaked into the atmosphere.

The TMI accident caused no immediate deaths or injuries, and later official investigations and reports concluded that the level of radioactivity was too low to have caused any significant health effects. A number of independent studies also have found that no related rise in cancer deaths has occurred among residents living near the TMI site in the years since the accident. Some local residents disputed these findings, however, reporting symptoms of high-dosage radiation poisoning, the death of pets and farm animals, and plant anomalies. Subsequent studies and health surveys have documented the residents' claims and at least one respected researcher, epidemiologist Steven Wing, found correlations between TMI radiation and increased rates of cancer among residents who lived downwind from the nuclear plant. Many critics believe, therefore, that radiation doses were much higher than official reports have suggested.

Seven years after the TMI incident, on April 25, 1986, a far more disastrous accident happened at the Chernobyl nuclear power plant in Ukraine. This accident has been widely attributed to human error and poor facility design. Workers at Chernobyl were testing the nuclear reactor and when they tried to return it to full power, they pulled the control rods out of the core too quickly, causing a rapid fission reaction called supercritical. Unlike nuclear reactors in the United States, which are required to be built with massive containment walls, the Soviet reactor had little protection around it. As a result, when the reactor violently exploded, it spewed radioactive materials and flames high into the sky and onto large swaths of nearby land, houses, and crops for nine days. Radioactive particles were then carried by winds around the world. Even today, parts of Sweden, Finland, Scotland, and Ireland remain so contaminated that sheep cannot graze in these areas. In the spring and summer of 1986, 116,000 people from the Chernobyl area were evacuated to non-contaminated regions, and an additional 230,000 people were relocated in subsequent years. The accident was the worst nuclear disaster in world history and it released hundreds of times more radiation contamination than the atomic bombs dropped on Japan at the end of World War II.

The Chernobyl accident turned eight hundred square miles into a nuclear wasteland and the forced relocations disrupted many lives and caused severe mental stress for local residents. A total of forty-seven people, mostly rescue workers from the plant, died from acute radiation poisoning because they were so close to the burning reactor core. In addition, in later years, a dramatic spike in thyroid cancer among children in nearby areas occurred; between four thousand and five thousand children were diagnosed with the cancer between 1992 and 2002. So far, nine of these children have died, and according to the World Health Organization (WHO), more deaths could occur in the future. So far, however, WHO maintains that no other statistically significant rise in any other type of cancer has occurred as a result of the accident. Yet a United Nations report predicted the total death rate from Chernobyl could ultimately rise as high as four thousand. As in the case with TMI, however, critics have challenged official reports and claim that the Chernobyl incident had devastating health effects. A 2006 report by Greenpeace International, for example, found that 60,000 people have already died because of the accident, and that another 140,000 people may be added to the death list in the future.

Since these two nuclear disasters, many technological and safety improvements have been made in nuclear reactors to reduce the chance of another accident. In the United States, for example, the nuclear industry and the Nuclear Regulatory Commission (NRC) have instituted changes in plant design, enhanced emergency preparedness, improved the inspection process, and expanded regulatory oversight. In the Soviet Union, officials made technological changes, renovated reactors, and instituted safety regulations. Efforts have also been made on an international level to promote nuclear power plant safety.

Although no more nuclear disasters have occurred since Chernobyl, a number of minor accidents, several of which have resulted in the release of radioactive material, have happened. Advocates for nuclear power cite the lack of major accidents and claim that the nuclear industry is safe, while nuclear power critics still see nuclear energy as inherently unsafe for both humans and the environment. The viewpoints contained in this chapter illustrate the nature of this important debate.

Nuclear Power Reactors Are One of the Safest Ways to Produce Electricity

World Nuclear Association

World Nuclear Association is the international organization that promotes nuclear energy and supports the many companies that make up the global nuclear industry.

In the 1950s attention turned to harnessing the power of the atom in a controlled way, as demonstrated at Chicago in 1942 and subsequently for military research, and applying the steady heat yield to generate electricity. This naturally gave rise to concerns about accidents and their possible effects. In particular the scenario of loss of cooling which resulted in melting of the nuclear reactor core motivated studies on both the physical and chemical possibilities and the biological effects of any dispersed radioactivity.

Those responsible for nuclear power technology in the West devoted extraordinary effort to ensuring that a meltdown of the reactor core would not take place, since it was assumed that a meltdown of the core would create a major public hazard, and if uncontained, a tragic accident with likely fatalities.

In avoiding such accidents the industry has been outstandingly successful. In 12,000 cumulative reactor-years of commercial operation in 32 countries, there have been only two major accidents to nuclear power plants—Three Mile Island and Chernobyl, the latter being of little relevance outside the old Soviet bloc.

World Nuclear Association, "Safety of Nuclear Reactors," June 2008. www.world
-nuclear.org. Reproduced by permission.

No Danger of Dramatic Public Harm

It was not until the late 1970s that detailed analyses and large-scale testing, followed by the 1979 meltdown of the Three Mile Island reactor, began to make clear that even the worst possible accident in a conventional Western nuclear power plant or its fuel could not cause dramatic public harm. The industry still works hard to minimize the probability of a meltdown accident, but it is now clear that no one need fear a potential public health catastrophe.

In 12,000 cumulative reactor-years of commercial operation in 32 countries, there have been only two major accidents to nuclear power plants.

The decades-long test and analysis program showed that less radioactivity escapes from molten fuel than initially assumed, and that this radioactive material is not readily mobilized beyond the immediate internal structure. Thus, even if the containment structure that surrounds all modern nuclear plants were ruptured, it would still be highly effective in preventing escape of radioactivity.

It is the laws of physics and the properties of materials that preclude disaster, not the required actions by safety equipment or personnel. In fact, licensing approval now requires that the effects of any core melt accident must be confined to the plant itself, without the need to evacuate nearby residents.

The two significant accidents in the 50-year history of civil nuclear power generation are:

- Three Mile Island (USA 1979) where the reactor was severely damaged but radiation was contained and there were no adverse health or environmental consequences

- Chernobyl (Ukraine 1986) where the destruction of the reactor by steam explosion and fire killed 31 people

and had significant health and environmental consequences. The death toll has since increased to about
56. . . .

These two significant accidents occurred during more than
12,700 reactor-years of civil operation. Of all the accidents
and incidents, only the Chernobyl accident resulted in radiation doses to the public greater than those resulting from the
exposure to natural sources. Other incidents (and one
'accident') have been completely confined to the plant.

Apart from Chernobyl, no nuclear workers or members of
the public have ever died as a result of exposure to radiation
due to a commercial nuclear reactor incident. Most of the serious radiological injuries and deaths that occur each year
(two to four deaths and many more exposures above regulatory limits) are the result of large uncontrolled radiation
sources, such as abandoned medical or industrial equipment.
(There have also been a number of accidents in experimental
reactors and in one military plutonium-producing pile—at
Windscale, UK, in 1957—but none of these resulted in loss of
life outside the actual plant, or long-term environmental
contamination.)

---

*A nuclear accident in a Western-type reactor is now un-
derstood to have severe financial consequences for the
owner but will give rise to minimal off-site consequences.*

It should be emphasised that a commercial-type power reactor simply cannot under any circumstances explode like a
nuclear bomb.

The International Atomic Energy Agency (IAEA) was set
up by the United Nations in 1957. One of its functions was to
act as an auditor of world nuclear safety. It prescribes safety
procedures and the reporting of even minor incidents. Its role
has been strengthened since 1996. Every country which operates nuclear power plants has a nuclear safety inspectorate and
all of these work closely with the IAEA.

While nuclear power plants are designed to be safe in their operation and safe in the event of any malfunction or accident, no industrial activity can be represented as entirely risk-free. However, a nuclear accident in a Western-type reactor is now understood to have severe financial consequences for the owner but will give rise to minimal off-site consequences.

Achieving Safety: The Record So Far

Operational safety is a prime concern for those working in nuclear plants. Radiation doses are controlled by the use of remote handling equipment for many operations in the core of the reactor. Other controls include physical shielding and limiting the time workers spend in areas with significant radiation levels. These are supported by continuous monitoring of individual doses and of the work environment to ensure very low radiation exposure compared with other industries.

Concerning possible accidents, up to the early 1970s, some extreme assumptions were made about the possible chain of consequences. These gave rise to a genre of dramatic fiction in the public domain and also some solid conservative engineering including containment structures (at least in Western reactor designs) in the industry itself. Licensing regulations were framed accordingly.

One mandated safety indicator is the calculated probable frequency of degraded core or core melt accidents. The U.S. Nuclear Regulatory Commission (NRC) specifies that reactor designs must meet a 1 in 10,000 year core damage frequency, but modern designs exceed this. US utility requirements are 1 in 100,000 years, the best currently operating plants are about 1 in 1 million and those likely to be built in the next decade are almost 1 in 10 million.

Even months after the Three Mile Island accident in 1979 it was assumed that there had been no core melt because there were no indications of severe radioactive release even inside the containment. It turned out that in fact about half the core had melted. This remains the only core melt in a reactor conforming to NRC safety criteria, and the effects were contained as designed, without radiological harm to anyone.

However, apart from this accident and the Chernobyl disaster there have been about ten core melt accidents—mostly in military or experimental reactors. . . . None resulted in any hazard outside the plant from the core melting, though in one case there was significant radiation release due to burning graphite.

Regulatory requirements today are that the effects of any core melt accident must be confined to the plant itself, without the need to evacuate nearby residents.

The use of nuclear energy for electricity generation can be considered extremely safe.

The main safety concern has always been the possibility of an uncontrolled release of radioactive material, leading to contamination and consequent radiation exposure off-site. Earlier assumptions were that this would be likely in the event of a major loss of cooling accident which resulted in a core melt. Experience has proved otherwise in any circumstances relevant to Western reactor designs. In the light of better understanding of the physics and chemistry of material in a reactor core under extreme conditions it became evident that even a severe core melt coupled with breach of containment could not in fact create a major radiological disaster from any Western reactor design. Studies of the post-accident situation at Three Mile Island supported this.

It has long been asserted that nuclear reactor accidents are the epitome of low-probability but high-consequence risks. Understandably, with this in mind, some people were disinclined to accept the risk, however low the probability. However, the physics and chemistry of a reactor core, coupled with but not wholly depending on the engineering, mean that the consequences of an accident are likely in fact to be much less severe than those from other industrial and energy sources. Experience bears this out.

At Chernobyl the kind of reactor and its burning graphite which dispersed radionuclides far and wide tragically meant that the results were severe. This once and for all vindicated the desirability of designing with inherent safety supplemented by robust secondary safety provisions and avoiding that kind of reactor design.

Mention should be made of the accident to the US Fermi 1 prototype fast breeder reactor near Detroit in 1966. Due to a blockage in coolant flow, some of the fuel melted. However, no radiation was released off-site and no one was injured. The reactor was repaired and restarted but closed down in 1972.

To achieve optimum safety, nuclear plants in the Western world operate ... with multiple safety systems supplementing the natural features of the reactor core.

The use of nuclear energy for electricity generation can be considered extremely safe. Every year several thousand people die in coal mines to provide this widely used fuel for electricity. There are also significant health and environmental effects arising from fossil fuel use. . . .

Achieving Optimum Nuclear Safety

To achieve optimum safety, nuclear plants in the Western world operate using a 'defence-in-depth' approach, with multiple safety systems supplementing the natural features of the reactor core. Key aspects of the approach are:

- high-quality design & construction

- equipment which prevents operational disturbances developing into problems

- redundant and diverse systems to detect problems, control damage to the fuel and prevent significant radioactive releases

- provision to confine the effects of severe fuel damage to the plant itself.

The safety provisions include a series of physical barriers between the radioactive reactor core and the environment, the provision of multiple safety systems, each with backup and designed to accommodate human error. Safety systems account for about one-quarter of the capital cost of such reactors.

The barriers in a typical plant are: the fuel is in the form of solid ceramic pellets, and radioactive fission products remain bound inside these pellets as the fuel is burned. The pellets are packed inside sealed zirconium alloy tubes to form fuel rods. These are confined inside a large steel pressure vessel with walls up to 30 cm thick—the associated primary water cooling pipe work is also substantial. All this, in turn, is enclosed inside a robust reinforced concrete containment structure with walls at least one metre thick.

But the main safety features of most reactors are inherent—negative temperature coefficient and negative void coefficient. The first means that beyond an optimal level, as the temperature increases the efficiency of the reaction decreases. The second means that if any steam has formed in the cooling water there is a decrease in moderating effect so that fewer neutrons are able to cause fission and the reaction slows down automatically.

Beyond the control rods which are inserted to absorb neutrons and regulate the fission process, the main engineered safety provisions are the backup emergency core cooling system to remove excess heat and the containment.

Traditional reactor safety systems are 'active' in the sense that they involve electrical or mechanical operation on command. Some engineered systems operate passively, e.g., pressure relief valves. Both require parallel redundant systems. Inherent or full passive safety design depends only on physical phenomena such as convection, gravity or resistance to high temperatures, not on functioning of engineered components. All reactors have some elements of inherent safety as mentioned above, but in some recent designs the passive or inherent features substitute for active systems in cooling, etc.

The basis of design assumes a threat where due to accident or malign intent (e.g., terrorism) there is core melting and a breach of containment. This double possibility has been well studied and provides the basis of exclusion zones and contingency plans. Apparently during the Cold War neither Russia nor the USA targeted the other's nuclear power plants because the likely damage would be modest.

There is a great deal of international cooperation on nuclear safety issues.

Nuclear power plants are designed with sensors to shut them down automatically in an earthquake, and this is a vital consideration in many parts of the world.

The Three Mile Island accident in 1979 demonstrated the importance of the inherent safety features. Despite the fact that about half of the reactor core melted, radionuclides released from the melted fuel mostly plated out on the inside of the plant or dissolved in condensing steam. The containment building which housed the reactor further prevented any significant release of radioactivity. The accident was attributed to mechanical failure and operator confusion. The reactor's other protection systems also functioned as designed. The emergency core cooling system would have prevented any damage to the reactor but for the intervention of the operators.

Investigations following the accident led to a new focus on the human factors in nuclear safety. No major design changes were called for in Western reactors, but controls and instrumentation were improved and operator training was overhauled.

By way of contrast, the Chernobyl reactor did not have a containment structure like those used in the West or in post-1980 Soviet designs. . . .

International Efforts to Improve Safety

There is a great deal of international cooperation on nuclear safety issues, in particular the exchange of operating experience under the auspices of the World Association of Nuclear Operators (WANO) which was set up in 1989. In practical terms this is the most effective international means of achieving very high levels of safety through its four major programs: peer reviews; operating experience; technical support and exchange; and professional and technical development. WANO peer reviews are the main proactive way of sharing experience and expertise. . . .

The IAEA Convention on Nuclear Safety was drawn up during a series of expert-level meetings from 1992 to 1994 and was the result of considerable work by governments, national nuclear safety authorities and the IAEA secretariat. Its aim is to legally commit participating states operating land-based nuclear power plants to maintain a high level of safety by setting international benchmarks to which states would subscribe.

The obligations of the parties are based to a large extent on the principles contained in the IAEA safety fundamentals document *The Safety of Nuclear Installations*. These obligations cover for instance, siting, design, construction, operation, the availability of adequate financial and human resources, the assessment and verification of safety, quality assurance and emergency preparedness.

The convention is an incentive instrument. It is not designed to ensure fulfillment of obligations by parties through control and sanction, but is based on their common interest to achieve higher levels of safety. These levels are defined by international benchmarks developed and promoted through regular meetings of the parties. The convention obliges parties to report on the implementation of their obligations for international peer review. This mechanism is the main innovative and dynamic element of the convention.

The convention entered into force in October 1996. As of April 2007, there were 65 signatories to the convention and 60 contracting parties. All countries with operating nuclear power plants are now among the 41 parties to the convention.

In relation to Eastern Europe particularly, since the late 1980s a major international program of assistance has been carried out by the OECD [Organisation for Economic Co-operation and Development], IAEA and [European] Commission . . . to bring early Soviet-designed reactors up to near Western safety standards, or at least to effect significant improvements to the plants and their operation. The European Union [EU] has also brought pressure to bear, particularly in countries which aspired to EU membership. . . .

Later Soviet-designed reactors are very much safer and the most recent ones have Western control systems or the equivalent, along with containment structures.

In 1996 the Convention on Nuclear Safety came into force. It is the first international legal instrument on the safety of nuclear power plants worldwide. It commits participating countries to maintain a high level of safety by setting international benchmarks to which they subscribe and against which they report. It has 65 signatories and has been ratified by 41 states.

Nuclear Energy Has Been Used Safely for Decades

American Energy Independence

American Energy Independence is an Internet-based publisher of articles and current news about American energy independence.

Although nuclear fusion is not available at this time, nuclear energy from nuclear fission is available today.

Nuclear fission creates no air pollution, but it does create a small amount of radioactive by-products. Opponents of nuclear energy believe a nuclear power plant accident would cause toxic radioactive nuclear material to be released into the environment. Fear of exposure to nuclear radiation has created public opposition to nuclear energy.

However, even with the potential danger of nuclear radiation, nuclear energy technology has a long history of safe operation. Worldwide nuclear electricity has accumulated over 10,000 reactor-years of operating experience. Today, the issue of nuclear energy safety and nuclear waste disposal is not a technical problem but one of public and political acceptance.

How Toxic Is Nuclear Radiation?

[According to nuclear engineer James Hopf,] "The direct radiation effect is the one thing that is different about nuclear material, as compared to other toxins, which may be the source of some of the fear and mystique. All other toxins require ingestion or inhalation for harm to occur. Radioactive material is the only toxin that can strike from a distance. This is because chemical toxins need to be in the body to cause chemi-

American Energy Independence, "Safe Nuclear Energy," 2009. www.americanenergy independence.com. Reproduced by permission.

cal changes that harm cells and biological processes, whereas radioactive material emits high energy particles that can travel over distances.". . .

Nuclear energy technology has a long history of safe operation.

"However . . . direct radiation will never be a significant factor with respect to total public health impact. Instead, the effects would come from dispersal of radioisotopes onto the land, air, and water, and the subsequent ingestion or inhalation of those isotopes. In all cases, the concentrations of radioisotopes would be far too small for the soil, water, or air in question to cause a significant direct radiation dose to a nearby person. However, if the radioactive isotopes are ingested or inhaled, and they then spend a significant residence time in the body, they will cause the adverse health effects that the public fears. But in this respect, radioactive material does not behave any differently from any other toxin. It basically has to be inhaled or ingested to have effect. . . . Thus, although the mystique exists, it will never come into play in any real way, in any real situations."

Most Americans Believe Nuclear Energy Is Safe

Nearly Seven of 10 Americans Favor Nuclear Energy: Public favorability of nuclear energy as one of the sources of electricity has exceeded 60 percent since 2001. In a September 2006 survey, 68 percent favor nuclear energy; 27 percent oppose.

A second national survey taken in March 2009 by Bisconti Research, Inc. found that 70 percent of Americans favor nuclear energy, with the number of Americans voicing strong support exceeding those strongly opposed by a margin of more than two to one.

"The strong public support shown for nuclear energy—and the fact that support is being sustained at levels as high as they have been in the 26 years that I have been conducting public opinion research on this topic—indicates a real change. The levels of support found for nuclear energy in recent months really are unprecedented," said Bisconti Research President Ann Bisconti.

Opposition to nuclear energy comes from a small but vocal minority of the American public.

"The poll found that the public is more concerned today about jobs, economic growth and energy independence than about global warming and air pollution. Clearly though, they see nuclear power as one of the ways to address all these challenges."

Opposition to nuclear energy comes from a small but vocal minority of the American public. Opponents of nuclear energy threaten lawsuits and political action against electric power companies. For this reason, electric power companies in the United States have not ordered a new nuclear power plant in 30 years.

If the American people fail to communicate their support for nuclear energy to their legislators, the opponents of nuclear energy will continue to stop new power plants from being built. If the opponents of nuclear energy continue to block the construction of nuclear power plants, there will be no future for nuclear engineers in America. Universities will stop offering nuclear engineering courses and the United States will fall behind the technology. America is at risk of losing its nuclear engineering expertise.

The antinuclear protesters are irrational, says [Dr. Robert L. DuPont] a psychiatrist and expert on fears and phobias who has studied and analyzed social perceptions of nuclear energy. . . .

DuPont is a practicing psychiatrist and a clinical professor of psychiatry at Georgetown University School of Medicine. He is also the author of *The Selfish Brain: Learning from Addiction* and *Nuclear Phobia—Phobic Thinking About Nuclear Power: A Discussion with Robert L. DuPont.*

The World Needs Nuclear Power

Nuclear energy is the only proven technology that can deliver baseload electricity on a large scale, 24 hours a day, 7 days a week, regardless of the weather, without producing carbon dioxide emissions. Nuclear power plants emit no carbon pollution—no carbon monoxide, no sulfur oxides and no nitrogen oxides to the atmosphere. And, nuclear power plants will not contaminate streams and rivers with mercury.

The United States now burns 400 million more tons of coal per year than was burned in 1980, because the United States stopped building nuclear power plants after the Three Mile Island nuclear reactor meltdown in 1979, even though no one was hurt, and the radiation was contained. There was no physical harm to public health; although antinuclear groups continue to inflict psychological harm on the public. . . .

Nuclear energy is the only proven technology that can deliver baseload electricity on a large scale, 24 hours a day, 7 days a week, . . . without producing carbon dioxide emissions.

We need nuclear power, says James Lovelock, the man who inspired the [European] Greens [a political party, environmental movement]. "We reject nuclear energy with the same unreasoning arguments that our ancestors would have used to reject geothermal energy, the effort to harness the heat of the earth. Compared with the imaginary dangers of nuclear power, the threat from the intensifying greenhouse effect seems all too real. I wholly support the Greens' wish to see all energy eventually come from renewable sources but I do not think that we have the time to wait until this happens. Nuclear power is unpopular but it is safer than power from fossil fuel. The worst that could happen, if Chernobyls become endemic, is that we live a little less long in a mildly radioactive world. To me this is preferable to the loss of our hard-won civilization in a greenhouse catastrophe.

"Nuclear electricity is now a well-tried and soundly engineered practice that is both safe and economical; given the will it could be applied quickly. It is risky if improperly used but even taking the Chernobyl disaster into account, it is, according to a recent Swiss study, by far the safest of the power industries. Disinformation about its dangers sustains a climate of fearful ignorance and has artificially inflated the difficulties of disposing of nuclear waste and the cost of nuclear power. If permitted, I would happily store high-level waste on my own land and use the heat from it to warm my home. There seems no sensible reason why nuclear waste should not be disposed of in the deep subducting regions of the ocean where tectonic forces draw all deposits down into the magma.

"What stands against the use of nuclear power is not sensible scientific or economic arguments but a widespread, unjustified, public fear. . . . The Greens, have so frightened their supporters that a change of mind would be almost impossible.

"The accident at Chernobyl is almost always presented as if it were the greatest industrial disaster of the 20th century. Even the BBC, in a recent programme, stated that thousands had died there. Such exaggeration suspends rational thought and is an unnerving triumph of fiction over science. In fact, 45 died at Chernobyl, according to the UN [United Nations] report on the disaster, and many of them were the firemen and helicopter crews who tried to extinguish the fire. It was an awful event and should never have happened, but it was far less lethal than the smog of 1952, when 5,000 Londoners died from poisoning by coal smoke." . . .

In recent years, a growing number of environmentalists have taken a new look at the safety record and benefits of nuclear energy:

[As Corinna Wu, of the American Society for Engineering Education's *Prism* magazine, explained in a 2006 article,] "Stewart Brand is a self-professed 'greenie.' an original hippie of the 1960s and founder of the *Whole Earth Catalog*, he has spent decades promoting environmental and social causes. So it came as a shock to many when last year [2008], Brand wrote an essay for *Technology Review* in which he touted the benefits of nuclear power. In the piece, titled 'Environmental Heresies,' Brand embraced nuclear as the only technology currently available that can help save the planet from global warming.

Nuclear fission is a sustainable source of energy.

"Soon, people began mentioning Brand with other prominent environmentalists who had also spoken in favor of nuclear: scientist James Lovelock, who proposed the Gaia hypothesis; Patrick Moore, cofounder of Greenpeace; and Anglican bishop Hugh Montefiore, a former board member of Friends of the Earth. According to Brand, others are following suit. 'I'm seeing much less resistance from my fellow greenies,' he said at a forum held at MIT [Massachusetts Institute of Technology] in September. 'Not total conversion, but fewer opposing it.'

"Nuclear is getting a second look from environmentalists because, unlike coal, natural gas and other fossil fuels, it does not produce carbon dioxide as a by-product. Carbon dioxide released into the atmosphere traps heat radiating from the earth's surface, thus leading to a gradual rise in global temperature. Scientific and governmental bodies around the world agree that much of the warming of the planet seen in the last

50 years is due to this kind of human activity, including the burning of fossil fuels for energy."

The Benefits of Nuclear Power

[As authors Richard Rhodes and Denis Beller explain,] "The great advantage of nuclear power is its ability to wrest enormous energy from a small volume of fuel. Nuclear fission, transforming matter directly to energy, is several million times as energetic as chemical burning, which merely breaks chemical bonds. One ton of nuclear fuel produces energy equivalent to 2 to 3 million tons of fossil fuel.... Running a 1,000 megawatt (a continuous 1 million kilowatt) power plant for a year requires 2,000 train cars of coal or 10 supertankers of oil but only 12 cubic meters of natural uranium.... The spent nuclear fuel and other radioactive waste requiring disposal after one year would be about 20 cubic meters in all when compacted (roughly, the volume of two automobiles).... The high-level waste is intensely radioactive, of course.... But thanks to its small volume and the fact that it is not released into the environment, this high-level waste can be meticulously sequestered behind multiple barriers. Waste from coal, dispersed across the landscape in smoke or buried near the surface, remains toxic forever. Radioactive nuclear waste decays steadily, losing 99 percent of its toxicity after 600 years—well within the range of human experience.... Nuclear waste disposal is a political problem in the United States because of widespread fear disproportionate to the reality of risk. But it is not an engineering problem." ...

By all practical definitions, nuclear fission is a sustainable source of energy. Enough uranium exists in the earth's crust and oceans to last thousands of years. Future advanced fast reactors will produce 60 to 100 times more energy out of the uranium fuel, extending the reserves to tens of thousands of years.

Is there enough uranium to supply a world dependent on nuclear energy? Yes, says nuclear engineer James Hopf, "the actual recoverable uranium supply is likely to be enough to last several hundred (up to 1,000) years, even using standard reactors. With breeders (advanced fast reactors), it is essentially infinite. Hundreds of thousands of years is certainly enough time to develop fusion power, or renewable sources that can meet all our power needs."...

Thirty percent of all USA CO_2 emissions are created when fossil fuels are burned to produce the nation's electricity. The replacement of coal power plants with nuclear power plants would reduce America's atmospheric CO_2 emissions by 30 percent.

Nuclear energy can replace power plants that burn coal, gas or oil. And, nuclear energy can help the USA develop a replacement for its petroleum-based transportation fuel.

Nuclear energy can provide the process heat and hydrogen gas require for the manufacture of synthetic fuels from coal. If nuclear heat and nuclear-generated hydrogen are used to produce synthetic fuels from coal, then the yield of synthetic fuel from coal would be much higher than if the coal is used to provide the process heat and hydrogen, resulting in much less CO_2 being released in the process.

If coal power plants were replaced by nuclear power plants, for baseload electricity, and coal is then used to make synthetic fuels, Americans who are dependent on the coal mining industry for their incomes would support nuclear energy. Today, the USA burns about 1 billion tons of coal per year in power plants. Using 1 billion tons of coal to produce synthetic fuel would replace 65 percent of America's imported oil. (At 12 million imported barrels per day, 65 percent is 7,800,000 barrels per day.) Just over 20 percent of oil imported into the USA today comes from Persian Gulf nations, which are also members of OPEC [Organization of the Petroleum Exporting

Countries]. Less than 45 percent of oil imported into the USA today comes from OPEC countries.

The United States has an estimated 270 billion tons of re-coverable coal in existing mines, having more than four times as much energy in coal than the Middle East has in oil—enough to last the United States a couple of centuries or more. That's only the coal in existing mines. If you consider total re-coverable reserves, the United States has over 500 billion tons of coal available to replace imported oil.

Nuclear Hydrogen for Production of Liquid Hydrocarbon Transport Fuels: [As Charles Forsberg of Oak Ridge National Laboratory explains,] "Liquid fuels (gasoline, diesel, and jet fuel) have major advantages as transport fuels: a high energy density per unit volume and mass, ease of storage, and ease of transport. However, there are major disadvantages: Crude oil is increasingly expensive, most of the world's crude oil comes from unstable parts of the world, and burning of hydrocar-bons releases greenhouse gases into the atmosphere. These disadvantages may be reduced or eliminated by use of hydro-gen and oxygen produced from water using nuclear energy as the energy source, and by use of alternative carbon feedstocks in the production of liquid fuels.

"As oil becomes scarce, liquid fuels will be produced with increasing frequency from heavier feedstocks such as heavy oil, tar sands, oil shale, and coal. With current technology, this conversion process can be summarized as follows: Carbon-based feedstock + Water + Oxygen—> Liquid fuels + Car-bon dioxide (1). With nuclear hydrogen, this conversion pro-cess can become: Carbon-based feedstock + Water + Nuclear energy—> Liquid fuels (2).

"When nuclear energy is used (Equation 2), no carbon di-oxide is released from the fuel production process. All the car-bon is incorporated into the fuel. The carbon in the feedstock is not used as an energy source in the liquid-fuel production process. Carbon dioxide is released only from the burning of the liquid fuels. For feedstocks such as coal, which have low hydrogen-to-carbon ratios, the traditional technologies such as coal liquefaction (Equation 1) may release more carbon dioxide to the environment in the fuel production process than will be released from burning the liquid fuel.

"Hydrocarbon liquid fuels that have no greenhouse impacts can be produced if the carbon source for the manufacture of the liquid fuels is carbon recycled from the atmosphere. With nuclear hydrogen production, this conversion process becomes: Recycle carbon + Water + Nuclear energy—> Liquid fuels (No greenhouse)." . . .

Nuclear Waste

It has been suggested that the Yucca Mountain repository [a proposed nuclear waste storage site in Nevada] should be regarded as a strategic uranium reserve, insuring that the spent fuel stored in the repository is retrievable for future generations of Americans. Light water reactors (LWRs) consume less than 2 percent of the potential energy within their uranium fuel. If, sometime in the near future, all of the "spent fuel" from the LWRs is reprocessed and made into new fuel for nuclear power plants, then Yucca Mountain will not be a radioactive problem 10,000 years from now. . . .

By recycling spent fuel, . . . a fast reactor system can deliver 100 times more energy from available uranium resources than today's reactors.

[As John K. Sutherland, chief scientist of Edutech Enterprises,] "The volume of the entire world's spent nuclear fuel (air spaces, shielding and cladding removed) for a year—assuming a specific gravity of about eight—is less than 2,000 cubic metres, which is about the internal volume of my modest home (10 metres by 20 by 10). No wonder there is no immediate need to do anything with it. And, it is also NOT waste, but represents a recyclable resource as only about 1 to 3 percent of the contained energy is used in the first pass through the reactor cycle. Store it retrievably, and we will eventually use it for the remaining energy content." . . .

[Sutherland also states,] "Marie Curie, one of the early pioneers of radioactive research and the winner of two Nobel Prizes, recognized the social value of dispelling ignorance, when she stated: 'Nothing is to be feared. It is to be understood'. Marie Curie herself was so radioactive from her 'bucket chemistry', and inhaling radon and ingesting radium and other nuclides, that when she entered any physics laboratory, it was noted that any charged electroscopes immediately lost their charge. She died, possibly of leukemia, at age 66, having outlived most of her generation. Nuclear wastes must surely be one of the most difficult and thorny topics to address in the complete absence of perspective, which is the way they are usually addressed. The general belief seems to be that only nuclear wastes are dangerous or socially damaging not only now, but also into the far distant future, and that wastes from other sources of energy are not. This general lack of perspective, and inability to compare social risks today and over time, is not only unnerving, but also expensive and hazardous to society's continued health.

"The issues of nuclear power, radiation, and nuclear wastes are rife with ignorance, political manipulation, environmental obfuscation, and fear. As a result, they are either a political minefield, or a gold mine of emotions, depending upon which side of these politicized issues you stand." . . .

Advanced Nuclear Fuel Cycle: Next generation nuclear reactors with a pyroprocessing-based fuel cycle can provide a vast improvement in energy efficiency. By recycling spent fuel, such a fast reactor system can deliver 100 times more energy from available uranium resources than today's reactors without harmful greenhouse gas emissions, thereby assuring a sustainable long-term energy source.

The Closed Fuel Cycle: A closed fuel cycle reprocesses spent reactor fuel to extract uranium and plutonium, the main elements that power the reactor. The alternative is to place spent fuel in repositories without reprocessing. Some closed fuel cycles, such as [Argonne National Laboratory's] pyroprocessing technology, extract minor actinides—waste elements such as neptunium and americium that take hundreds of thousands of years to decay—along with uranium and plutonium and recycle them all into new fuel. The reactor destroys the actinides by fission as it generates electricity. With the actinides gone, the short-lived wastes need environmental isolation for less than 1,000 years. "In that time," said John Sackett, Argonne associate laboratory director for engineering research, "they decay until they are less radioactive than the natural ore the original fuel came from. You'd still need repositories, but you'd have less material to fill them, and they would be less costly to build and maintain."

Nuclear Energy Risks Are Inconsequential

Bernard L. Cohen

Bernard L. Cohen is an author and a professor emeritus of physics and astronomy and of environmental and occupational health at the University of Pittsburgh in Pennsylvania.

The principal risks associated with nuclear power arise from health effects of radiation. This radiation consists of subatomic particles traveling at or near the velocity of light— 186,000 miles per second. They can penetrate deep inside the human body where they can damage biological cells and thereby initiate a cancer. If they strike sex cells, they can cause genetic diseases in progeny.

Radiation occurs naturally in our environment; a typical person is, and always has been struck by 15,000 particles of radiation every second from natural sources, and an average medical X-ray involves being struck by 100 billion. While this may seem to be very dangerous, it is not, because the probability for a particle of radiation entering a human body to cause a cancer or a genetic disease is only one chance in 30 million billion (30 quintillion).

Risks from Nuclear Power Are Small

Nuclear power technology produces materials that are active in emitting radiation and are therefore called "radioactive." These materials can come into contact with people . . . through small releases during routine plant operation, accidents in nuclear power plants, accidents in transporting radioactive materials, and escape of radioactive wastes from confinement systems. We will discuss these separately, but all of them taken

Bernard L. Cohen, "Risks of Nuclear Power," Physics Department at Idaho State University, accessed October 23, 2009. www.physics.isu.edu. Reproduced by permission.

together, with accidents treated probabilistically, will eventually expose the average American to about 0.2% of his exposure from natural radiation. Since natural radiation is estimated to cause about 1% of all cancers, radiation due to nuclear technology should eventually increase our cancer risk by 0.002% (one part in 50,000), reducing our life expectancy by less than one hour. By comparison, our loss of life expectancy from competitive electricity generation technologies, burning coal, oil, or gas, is estimated to range from 3 to 40 days.

Radiation due to nuclear technology should eventually increase our cancer risk by 0.002% (one part in 50,000), reducing our life expectancy by less than one hour.

There has been much misunderstanding on genetic diseases due to radiation. The risks are somewhat less than the cancer risks; for example, among the Japanese A-bomb survivors from Hiroshima and Nagasaki, there have been about 400 extra cancer deaths among the 100,000 people in the follow-up group, but there have been no extra genetic diseases among their progeny. Since there is no possible way for the cells in our bodies to distinguish between natural radiation and radiation from the nuclear industry, the latter cannot cause new types of genetic diseases or deformities (e.g., bionic man), or threaten the "human race." Other causes of genetic disease include delayed parenthood (children of older parents have higher incidence) and men wearing pants (this warms the gonads, increasing the frequency of spontaneous mutations). The genetic risks of nuclear power are equivalent to delaying parenthood by 2.5 days, or of men wearing pants an extra 8 hours per year. Much can be done to avert genetic diseases utilizing currently available technology; if 1% of the taxes paid by the nuclear industry were used to further implement this technology, 80 cases of genetic disease would be averted for each case caused by the nuclear industry.

Reactor Accidents

The nuclear power plant design strategy for preventing accidents and mitigating their potential effects is "defense in depth"—if something fails, there is a backup system to limit the harm done, if that system should also fail there is another backup system for it, etc., etc. Of course, it is possible that each system in this series of backups might fail one after the other, but the probability for that is exceedingly small. The media often publicize a failure of some particular system in some plant, implying that it was a "close call" on disaster; they completely miss the point of defense in depth, which easily takes care of such failures. Even in the Three Mile Island accident where at least two equipment failures were severely compounded by human errors, two lines of defense were still not breached—essentially all of the radioactivity remained sealed in the thick steel reactor vessel, and that vessel was sealed inside the heavily reinforced concrete and steel lined "containment" building that was never even challenged. It was clearly not a close call on disaster to the surrounding population. The Soviet Chernobyl reactor, built on a much less safe design concept, did not have such a containment structure; if it did, that disaster would have been averted.

Risks from reactor accidents are estimated by the rapidly developing science of "probabilistic risk analysis" (PRA). A PRA must be done separately for each power plant (at a cost of $5 million) but we give typical results here: A fuel meltdown might be expected once in 20,000 years of reactor operation. In 2 out of 3 meltdowns there would be no deaths, in 1 out of 5 there would be over 1,000 deaths, and in 1 out of 100,000 there would be 50,000 deaths. The average for all meltdowns would be 400 deaths. Since air pollution from coal burning is estimated to be causing 10,000 deaths per year, there would have to be 25 meltdowns each year for nuclear power to be as dangerous as coal burning.

The genetic risks of nuclear power are equivalent to delaying parenthood by 2.5 days, or of men wearing pants an extra 8 hours per year.

Of course deaths from coal burning air pollution are not noticeable, but the same is true for the cancer deaths from reactor accidents. In the worst accident considered, expected once in 100,000 meltdowns (once in 2 billion years of reactor operation), the cancer deaths would be among 10 million people, increasing their cancer risk typically from 20% (the current U.S. average) to 20.5%. This is much less than the geographical variation—22% in New England to 17% in the Rocky Mountain states.

Very high radiation doses can destroy body functions and lead to death within 60 days, but such "noticeable" deaths would be expected in only 2% of reactor meltdown accidents; there would be over 100 in 0.2% of meltdowns, and 3,500 in one out of 100,000 meltdowns. To date, the largest number of noticeable deaths from coal burning was in an air pollution incident (London, 1952) where there were 3,500 extra deaths in one week. Of course the nuclear accidents are hypothetical and there are many ... worse hypothetical accidents in other electricity generation technologies; e.g., there are hydroelectric dams in California whose sudden failure could cause 200,000 deaths.

Radioactive Waste

The radioactive waste products from the nuclear industry must be isolated from contact with people for very long time periods. The bulk of the radioactivity is contained in the spent fuel, which is quite small in volume and therefore easily handled with great care. This "high-level waste" will be converted to a rock-like form and emplaced in the natural habitat of rocks, deep underground. The average lifetime of a rock in that environment is 1 billion years. If the waste behaves like other rock, it is easily shown that the waste generated by one nuclear power plant will eventually, over millions of years (if there is no cure found for cancer), cause one death from 50 years of operation. By comparison, the wastes from coal-burning plants that end up in the ground will eventually cause several thousand deaths from generating the same amount of electricity.

The bulk of the radioactivity [from nuclear plants] is contained in the spent fuel, which is quite small in volume and therefore easily handled with great care.

The much larger volume of much less radioactive (low level) waste from nuclear plants will be buried at shallow depths (typically 20 feet) in soil. If we assume that this material immediately becomes dispersed through the soil between the surface and groundwater depth (despite elaborate measures to maintain waste package integrity) and behaves like the same materials that are present naturally in soil (there is extensive evidence confirming such behavior), the death toll from this low-level waste would be 5% of that from the high-level waste discussed in the previous paragraph.

Other Radiation Problems

The effects of routine releases of radioactivity from nuclear plants depend somewhat on how the spent fuel is handled. A typical estimate is that they may reduce our life expectancy by 15 minutes.

Potential problems from accidents in transport of radioactive materials are largely neutralized by elaborate packaging. A great deal of such transport has taken place over the past 50 years and there have been numerous accidents, including fatal ones. However, from all of these accidents combined, there is less than a 1% chance that even a single death will ever result from radiation exposure. Probabilistic risk analyses indicate that we can expect less than one death per century in the U.S. from this source.

Mining uranium to fuel nuclear power plants leaves "mill tailings," the residues from chemical processing of the ore, which lead to radon exposures to the public. However, these effects are grossly overcompensated by the fact that mining uranium out of the ground reduces future radon exposures. By comparison, coal burning leaves ashes that increase future radon exposures. The all-inclusive estimates of radon effects are that one nuclear power plant operating for one year will eventually *avert* a few hundred deaths, while an equivalent coal-burning plant will eventually *cause* 30 deaths.

Nuclear Power Plants Greatly Increase Cancer Rates

Samuel S. Epstein

Samuel S. Epstein is a professor emeritus of environmental and occupational health sciences at the University of Illinois at Chicago School of Public Health, chairman of the Cancer Prevention Coalition, and author of more than two hundred scientific articles and fifteen books on cancer.

Nuclear power, frequently mentioned as one option for meeting future energy needs, would pose a health threat to Americans if a meltdown occurred. But despite meltdowns at Chernobyl and Three Mile Island, and many other near miss accidents, there is another dirty little secret the nuclear industry doesn't want you to know. Cancer risk from nuclear plants aren't just *potential* risks, they are *actual* risks.

Every day, reactors must routinely release a portion of radioactive chemicals into local air and water—the same chemicals found in atomic bomb tests. They enter human bodies through breathing and the food chain. Federal law obligates nuclear companies to measure these emissions and the amounts that end up in air, water, and food, and to report them to federal regulators.

However, nuclear advocates consistently claim that these releases are below federally permitted limits, and thus are harmless. But this thinking is a leap that ignores hard evidence from scientific studies. Now, after half a century of a large-scale experiment with nuclear power, the verdict is in: Nuclear reactors cause cancer.

Samuel S. Epstein, "Nuclear Power Causes Cancer: What Industry Doesn't Want You to Know," Huffington Post, August 4, 2009. www.huffingtonpost.com. Reproduced by permission of the author.

Government on the Sidelines

The claim that low doses of radiation are harmless has always been just a claim. It led to practices like routine diagnostic X-rays to the pelvis of pregnant women, until the work of the University of Oxford's Dr. Alice Stewart found that these X-rays doubled the chance that the fetus would die of cancer as a child. Many studies later, independent experts agreed that no dose is safe. A 2005 report by a blue-ribbon panel of the National Academy of Sciences reviewed hundreds of scientific articles, and concluded that there is no risk-free dose of radiation.

After half a century of a large-scale experiment with nuclear power, the verdict is in: Nuclear reactors cause cancer.

Federal health officials, who should be responsible for tracking cancer near nuclear reactors and analyzing their nuclear contaminants, have ignored the dangers. The only national analysis of the topic was a 1990 study mandated by Senator Edward [Ted] Kennedy, and conducted by the National Cancer Institute. But this study was biased before it even got started. A January 28, 1988, letter to Senator Kennedy from National Institutes of Health director Dr. James Wyngaarden brazenly declared, "The most serious impact of the Three Mile Island accident that can be identified with certainty is mental stress to those living near the plant, particularly pregnant women and families with teenagers and young children." Not surprisingly, the study concluded there was no evidence of high cancer rates near reactors. No updated study has since been conducted by federal officials.

With government on the sidelines, it has been up to independent researchers—publishing results in medical and scientific journals—to generate the needed evidence. Studies were limited until the 1990s, but the few publications consistently documented high local cancer rates near reactors. Dr. Richard Clapp of Boston University found high leukemia rates near the Pilgrim plant in Massachusetts. Colorado health official Dr. Carl Johnson documented high child cancer rates near the San Onofre plant in California.

Columbia University researchers showed that cancer cases within a 10-mile radius of the Three Mile Island plant soared 64% in the first five years after the 1979 meltdown. Following the federal government's party line, they claimed that "stress" rather than radiation caused this increase. But the cat was out of the bag. Dr. Steven Wing of the University of North Carolina published a paper using the same data confirming the radiation-cancer link.

Joseph Mangano, MPH, MBA, executive director of the Radiation and Public Health Project, has authored 23 scientific articles since the mid-1990s documenting high local cancer rates near nukes. One study showed child cancer exceeded the national rate near 14 of 14 plants in the eastern United States. Another showed that when U.S. nuclear plants closed, local infant deaths and child cancer cases plunged immediately after shutdown.

A November 2007 article on U.S. child leukemia deaths ... showed local rates rose as nuclear plants aged— except near plants that shut down.

Other publications by Mangano have shown rising levels of radioactive strontium-90, emitted by reactors, in baby teeth of children living near reactors, which were closely linked with trends in childhood cancer rates.

The young aren't the only ones affected by reactor emissions. New evidence has examined adult rates of thyroid cancer, a disease especially sensitive to radiation. Thyroid is the fastest-rising cancer in the United States, nearly tripling since 1980. This evidence proves that most U.S. counties with the highest thyroid cancer rates are within a 90-mile radius covering eastern Pennsylvania, New Jersey, and southern New York. This area has 16 nuclear reactors (13 still in operation) at 7 plants, the densest concentration of reactors in the United States.

A November 2007 article on U.S. child leukemia deaths updated the 1990 National Cancer Institute study and showed local rates rose as nuclear plants aged—except near plants that shut down.

Better Government Studies Needed

A nationwide study of current cancer rates near nukes is sorely needed. In May this year [2009], the U.S. Nuclear Regulatory Commission (NRC) quietly announced it was commissioning an update of the 1990 National Cancer [Institute] study. This sounds like a positive step. However, the NRC has long been a harsh critic of any suggestion that reactors cause cancer. This is not surprising, since the commission receives 90% of its funds from nuclear companies that operate reactors.

Rather than ask for competitive bids for the cancer study, the NRC simply handed the job to the Oak Ridge Institute for Science and Education. Oak Ridge is an Energy Department contractor in the city that has operated a nuclear weapons plant for over half a century. The "Institute" is merely a front for pro-nuclear forces. It has no record of publishing scientific articles on cancer rates near reactors. The whitewash is on.

Several steps must be taken urgently. President [Barack] Obama, who will appoint replacements for 2 of the 5 NRC commissioners later this year, should select independent members—not the yes-men for the nuclear industry who have run the NRC for so many years. The NRC should bow out of the cancer study. Finally, Congress should appropriate funds supporting a truly independent study on cancer rates near U.S. reactors. The American public deserves to know just what these machines have done to them, so that future energy policies will better protect public health.

Human Fallibility Results in Nuclear Accidents

Robert Kyriakides

Robert Kyriakides is a qualified solicitor and chief executive of Genersys Plc, the United Kingdom's largest supplier of solar thermal panels.

Two events illustrating the potential danger of using nuclear energy have come to light recently, one in Plymouth in Devon and one in Thule, Greenland. Nuclear energy can be as safe as any other form of energy, in theory. The theory breaks down when the intervention of those imperfect creatures, human beings intercede. Accidents will happen.

In one case the nuclear energy was being used to propel a British submarine, HMS *Trafalgar*, which was based at the naval base on the deep River Tamar at Devonport. Coolant from the submarine was being transferred into an effluent tank at the quayside when a hose broke, discharging coolant into the Tamar. The coolant [is] used to transfer heat from the submarine coolant core to the tank. Once in the tank it would have been treated to reduce radioactivity. The Ministry of Defence say there has been no risk to the public. However, one wonders why, if the coolant was not radioactive, it had to go through a treatment process to reduce radioactivity.

Thousands of miles away, on the northwest coast of Greenland we have discovered an unwelcome nuclear legacy from 1968. Then a fire broke out on a U.S. B-52 bomber that caused the bomber to abandon three nuclear warheads. They crashed onto the ice and broke into pieces. The damage was cleared up from two of the bombs but the third bomb sunk through the ice into the bed of the sea. It has never been recovered. The U.S. government says we need not worry.

Robert Kyriakides, "Nuclear Energy—Accidents Will Happen," Robert Kyriakides's Weblog, November 13, 2008. http://robertkyriakides.wordpress.com. Reproduced by permission.

Some of the Danish workers involved in the cleanup who performed their jobs without protective clothing have developed illnesses related to plutonium exposure and are suing for damages. The missing bomb has never been found. If the U.S. military could not find it (and I am sure that they looked very hard for it) then I doubt if anyone else could find it, but the materials from which the bomb was made, particularly the casing, will not last forever and no doubt eventually the plutonium may leak into the sea, causing damage to the wildlife, an essential part of the food chain, which we humans end up eating, one way or another.

Accidents will happen, but in the case of a nuclear accident we have to decide—is it worth the risk when we can find other far less risky ways to generate . . . electricity?

Nuclear Accidents Will Happen

Accidents will happen. The best-laid schemes o' mice an' men gang aft agley [often go awry], as [poet] Robert Burns pointed out. So, when the government plans their new nuclear age of nuclear reactors to produce electricity for the nation, I am sure that safety will be a paramount consideration. But I am sure that the Navy planned its coolant transfer in Devonport as well as it could, and certainly the U.S. Air Force planned the safety of the B-52 bombers as well as they could, but in the end accidents did happen.

Unlike most other devices nuclear devices have some special factors.

- The danger of nuclear contamination is invisible and can only be detected with instruments.

- It is long-lasting—the dangers of nuclear accidents last thousands of years.

- Contamination can easily infect the food we eat, causing dreadful problems for animals and humans.

- The nuclear material can be relatively easily fashioned into one of the few genuine weapons of mass destruction that the world can produce.

Of course we need energy, but not at any cost. Accidents will happen, but in the case of a nuclear accident we have to decide—is it worth the risk when we can find other far less risky ways to generate the electricity that we use so greedily and selfishly?

Nuclear Energy Has Many Fatal Flaws

Public Citizen

Public Citizen is a national, nonprofit consumer advocacy organization that represents consumer interests in the legislative, judicial, and executive branches of government.

Nuclear power has made headlines recently as a possible player in the energy future of the United States, after decades of decline. But how do claims by industry and government champions stack up against the unsolved problems and dangers nuclear energy poses?

Cost

Despite its promise more than 50 years ago of energy "too cheap to meter," nuclear power continues to be dependent on taxpayer handouts to survive. From 1947 through 1999 the nuclear industry was given over $115 billion in direct taxpayer subsidies. Including Price-Anderson [Act] limitations on nuclear liability, the federal subsidies reach $145.4 billion. To put this in perspective, federal government subsidies for wind and solar [power] totaled $5.7 billion over the same period. The management of radioactive waste and the requirements for reactor decommissioning also require additional funds. Other aspects of nuclear power, such as the pollution from uranium mining, risks from nuclear weapons proliferation, dangers of reactor accidents, and the legacy of radioactive waste, are further hidden costs.

More Federal Subsidies. The high capital costs and long construction times of reactors make new reactors prohibitively expensive unless they are heavily subsidized by taxpayers. The

Public Citizen, "The Fatal Flaws of Nuclear Power," April, 2006. www.citizen.org. Reproduced by permission.

Energy Policy Act of 2005 contains over $13 billion dollars in new subsidies and tax breaks, as well as other incentives, for the nuclear industry, including:

- Reauthorization of the Price-Anderson Act, which limits industry liability in case of a severe accident; the rest of the tab would be picked up by taxpayers—possibly over $500 billion.

- More than $1 billion for research and development of new reactor designs and reprocessing technologies.

- Authorization of $2 billion in "risk insurance" to pay the industry for delays in construction and operation licensing for six new reactors, including delays due to the [U.S.] Nuclear Regulatory Commission or litigation.

- Authorization of more than $1.25 billion for the construction of a nuclear plant in Idaho.

- Tax credits for electricity production, estimated to cost $5.7 billion by 2025.

- Unlimited loan guarantees to back up to 80% of the cost of construction in case of default.

The high cost of nuclear power means that resources wasted on nuclear power take away from faster, cheaper, and cleaner solutions to climate change.

Even with these incentives, Standard & Poor's recently concluded that such subsidies "may not be enough to mitigate the risks associated with operating issues and high capital costs that could hinder credit quality."

Why Is Cost Important? With the limited amount of money available to spend on tackling global climate change, we need to obtain the greatest reduction in carbon emissions per dollar spent. The high cost of nuclear power means that resources wasted on nuclear power take away from faster, cheaper, and cleaner solutions to climate change.

Waste

Nuclear power is not a clean energy source. In fact, it produces both low- and high-level radioactive waste that remains dangerous for several hundred thousand years. Generated throughout all parts of the fuel cycle, this waste poses a serious danger to human health. Currently, over 2,000 metric tons of high-level radioactive waste and 12 million cubic feet of low-level radioactive waste are produced annually by the 103 operating reactors in the United States. *No country in the world has found a solution for this waste.* Building new nuclear plants would mean the production of much more of this dangerous waste with nowhere for it to go.

Uranium Mining and Processing. Uranium must be mined and enriched to form fuel for nuclear reactors. Each of these procedures results in radioactive contamination of the environment and risks to public health. Most uranium mining in the United States takes place in Utah, Colorado, New Mexico, Arizona, and Wyoming—areas of the country that are suffering from its effects. Uranium is mined by physically removing uranium ore, or by extracting the uranium in a newer process known as in-situ leaching. Conventional mining has caused dust and radon inhalation for workers—resulting in high rates of lung cancer and other respiratory diseases—and both types of mining have caused serious contamination of groundwater. When conventionally mined, uranium metal must be separated from the rock in a process called milling, which forms large radon-contaminated piles of material known as tailings. These tailings are often abandoned above ground. Twelve million tons of tailings, for instance, are piled along the Colorado River near Moab, Utah, threatening communities downstream. In the case of in-situ leaching, a solution is pumped into the ground to dissolve the uranium. When the mixture is returned to the surface, the uranium is separated and the remaining wastewater evaporated in slurry pools. Following this separation, uranium is sent to a facility for enrichment—a process that concentrates the amount of fissile uranium. Enrichment produces toxic hydrogen fluoride gas and large amounts of depleted uranium. Depleted uranium poses a threat to public health and should be disposed of in a geologic repository.

No country in the world has found a solution for [nuclear] waste.

Waste from Reactors. Over 54,000 metric tons of irradiated fuel have accumulated at the sites of commercial nuclear reactors in the United States. There are several proposals to manage this highly radioactive waste, but none of them would satisfactorily deal with the material.

Yucca Mountain. The Yucca Mountain project [a proposed waste storage site in Nevada] continues to be mired in controversy and may very well never open. Numerous unresolved problems remain with the geologic and hydrologic suitability of the proposed site, and serious questions have been raised about its ability to contain highly radioactive waste for the time required. In December 2004, the Department of Energy (DOE) missed its stated license application deadline for the project. DOE currently has no estimate of when it will submit its application. In July 2004, the D.C. Circuit Court of Appeals found that the time limit set by the Environmental Protection Agency (EPA) during which radiation in the groundwater at the site boundary must meet federal drinking water standards was inadequate and illegal. In August 2005, the EPA released a revised standard for the site. The proposed standard, however, still fails to safeguard public health, and would be the least protective radiation standard in the world.

Scientific fraud is also a long-standing problem in the research on the site. In March 2005, DOE and the U.S. Geological Survey [USGS] revealed e-mails showing that USGS scientists falsified data related to quality assurance and modeling of water infiltration at the site. Quality assurance (QA) is extremely important to good science, because QA procedures are established to ensure that the data are generated, documented, and reported correctly. The data in question deal with how rapidly water can travel through the mountain, corrode waste containers, and release the material into the environment. There have been other issues in the past with the movement of water through Yucca Mountain.

Private Fuel Storage. Private Fuel Storage (PFS) is a consortium of eight commercial nuclear utilities seeking to open an aboveground "interim" storage site for 40,000 metric tons of irradiated fuel on Goshute land in Utah. After an eight-year struggle, NRC granted the consortium a license in September 2005, but the license still requires the approval of the Bureau of Land Management and the Bureau of Indian Affairs. Three of the companies involved in the project have also recently withdrawn or decided to withhold funding from the consortium. If opened, PFS would not solve the waste problem, even temporarily. By transporting waste and storing it above ground in yet another part of the country, PFS will just make the existing waste problem worse. The "temporary" nature PFS is also questionable, because the project is completely dependent on the opening of Yucca Mountain. PFS raises serious environmental justice issues, because the lease with the Goshute tribe on which PFS is based is mired in controversy and corruption.

Reprocessing, Fast Reactors, and Transmutation. Fast reactors, in combination with reprocessing and transmutation, have also been proposed by the [George W.] Bush administration as a way to deal with the waste produced by nuclear power.

Specifically, fast neutron reactors—high temperature reactors that use separated plutonium and have an inert gas or liquid metal as a coolant—have been put forth as a way to reduce the radioactivity of the waste by converting long-lived radionuclides into shorter-lived radionuclides in a process known as transmutation. But fast neutron reactors have a terrible track record in safety and are incredibly expensive. These reactor designs also have many remaining technological problems, including the difficulties of using plutonium fuels in operating reactors, low rates of transmutation, unproven fuel fabrication systems, and dangers to workers making the fuel. Even if these problems were addressed, fast neutron reactors would not eliminate the need for a repository.

The U.S. Nuclear Regulatory Commission (NRC) and nuclear industry are leaving plants vulnerable [to terrorist attacks].

Reprocessing, the chemical process of extracting uranium and plutonium from irradiated fuel after it is removed from a reactor, also has problems. Reprocessing technology, which is an essential component of the fast reactor cycle, is extremely expensive, poses a security threat, leads to environmental contamination, and also does not eliminate the need for a repository.

Security

Nuclear plants currently operate at 64 sites in 31 states. Considering the devastation that could result from a successful terrorist attack on a nuclear plant, ensuring their protection should be a priority in a post–September 11 environment. However, the U.S. Nuclear Regulatory Commission (NRC) and nuclear industry are leaving plants vulnerable.

What Could Happen? The 9/11 Commission [a group put together to study the September 11, 2001, terrorist attacks] noted in June 2004 that al Qaeda's original plan for September 11 was to hijack 10 airplanes and crash two of them into nuclear plants. A September 2004 study by Dr. Ed Lyman of the Union of Concerned Scientists, using the NRC's own analysis method, found that a worst-case accident or attack at the Indian Point nuclear plant 35 miles north of New York City could cause up to 43,700 immediate fatalities and up to 518,000 long-term cancer deaths. Such a release could cost up to $2.1 trillion, and would force the permanent relocation of 11.1 million people.

Security Tests Still Inadequate. Between 1991 and 2001 almost half the plants tested failed to prevent mock attackers from simulating damage that would result in significant core damage and risk of meltdown—even though guards were defending against a group of only three attackers. After being suspended and revised following September 11, 2001, the new tests have less than double that number, according to *Time* magazine and other sources. That's far fewer than the 19 we have already experienced.

Safety

A 2002 survey of the NRC's workforce, commissioned by the NRC's Office of the Inspector General (OIG) and conducted by an independent contractor, revealed troubling facts about employees' confidence in the agency's ability to be an effective regulator. Many employees reported a concern that "NRC is becoming influenced by private industry and its power to regulate is diminishing." Meanwhile, only slightly more than half of NRC employees reported feeling that it is "safe to speak up in the NRC"—a finding that does not instill confidence in the NRC's ability to identify potential safety problems before they become serious.

At the Salem and Hope Creek nuclear plants in New Jersey, operated by PSEG Nuclear, serious mismanagement and a deficient safety culture in fact led to the deterioration of the physical condition of the plant—a situation brought to light by a whistle-blower who had been fired from her job as a manager at the plant allegedly for voicing safety concerns. Three independent assessments of the situation confirmed the problems at the plant, and an NRC review found "weaknesses in corrective actions and management efforts to establish an environment where employees are consistently willing to raise safety concerns." The NRC also found a general sentiment among employees of the plants that PSEG had emphasized production over safety.

Case Study: Davis-Besse. Mismanagement by FirstEnergy Nuclear Operating Company and lax oversight by the NRC allowed severe degradation of the nuclear reactor vessel head at the Davis-Besse nuclear plant in Oak Harbor, Ohio, to go unnoticed for years until it was finally discovered in March 2002 that a mere three-eighths of an inch of metal cladding was all that contained the essential coolant pressure boundary of the reactor vessel, a dire situation that could have easily led to a reactor breach, subsequent loss of coolant, and potential meltdown.

A December 2002 report by the NRC's Office of the Inspector General (OIG) found that the NRC's decision to allow the continued operation of Davis-Besse "was driven in large part by a desire to lessen the financial impact on [FirstEnergy Nuclear Operating Company] that would result from an early shutdown."

As more reactors are built around the world, nuclear material becomes more vulnerable to theft and diversion.

The OIG further concluded that the "NRC appears to have informally established an unreasonably high burden of requiring absolute proof of a safety problem, versus lack of reasonable assurance of maintaining public health and safety, before it will act to shut down a power plant."

Case Study: Tritium Leaks and Groundwater Contamination. The nuclear industry has also recently come under fire for leaking tritium—a radioactive isotope of hydrogen—into the groundwater of areas surrounding nuclear plants. Leaks have been reported at the Braidwood, Byron, and Dresden reactors in Illinois, the Palo Verde reactors in Arizona, and the Indian Point nuclear plant near New York City. Even worse, nuclear energy companies have kept the discoveries of these leaks from the public, sometimes for several years. Tritium is a by-product of nuclear generation and can enter the body through ingestion, absorption or inhalation. Long-term exposure can increase the risk of cancer, birth defects and genetic damage. In June 2005, the most recent study from the National Academy of Sciences (NAS) reaffirmed that there is no level of radiation exposure that is harmless or beneficial, and that even the smallest dose of ionizing radiation is capable of contributing to the development of cancer. Tritium takes about 250 years to decay to negligible levels, and is very difficult to remove from water.

Proliferation

Nuclear power also increases the risks of nuclear weapons proliferation. As more reactors are built around the world, nuclear material becomes more vulnerable to theft and diversion. Power reactors have also historically led directly to nuclear weapons programs in many countries.

Sensitive nuclear technology such as uranium enrichment and spent nuclear fuel reprocessing are ostensibly employed to create fuel in power reactors; they may be easily adjusted or redirected to produce weapons-grade fissile material. Moreover, power reactors themselves produce plutonium, which may be used in bombs. In practice, there is no way to segregate nuclear technologies employed for "peaceful" purposes from technologies that may be employed in weapons—the former may be, and have been, transformed into the latter.

Climate Change

The vast majority of public interest and environmental groups are adamantly opposed to nuclear power because it creates dangerous waste, brings unnecessary risks, and cannot rescue us from climate change. Over 300 national, state, and local organizations have endorsed a statement clearly outlining their reasons for continuing to oppose to nuclear power as a solution to climate change, while not a single environmental group is advocating for more nuclear plants. Nuclear power is too slow, expensive, and inflexible a technology to address climate change, and would entail the building of thousands of new nuclear reactors. These reactors would result in intensified proliferation, waste, and safety problems. These reactors would also drain investment away from renewable technologies. According to a new analysis by Public Citizen based on the work of governments, universities and other organizations in the United States, Europe and Japan, it is technically and economically feasible for a diverse mix of existing renewable technologies to completely meet U.S. energy needs over the coming decades. Clean, safe renewable energy sources—such as wind, solar, advanced hydroelectric and some types of biomass and geothermal energy—can reliably generate as much energy as conventional fuels without significant carbon emissions, destructive mining or the production of radioactive waste.

Nuclear Energy Wastes Resources and Threatens Health and Safety

Sherwood Ross

Sherwood Ross is a Miami-based reporter.

In all the annals of spin, few statements are as misleading as Vice President [Dick] Cheney's that the nuclear industry operates "efficiently, safely, and with no discharge of greenhouse gases or emissions," or President [George W.] Bush's claim that America's 103 nuclear plants operate "without producing a single pound of air pollution or greenhouse gases."

Even as the [George W. Bush] White House refuses to concede global warming is really happening, it touts nuclear power as the answer to it as if it were an arm of the Nuclear Energy Institute (NEI), the industry's trade group. NEI's advertisements declare, "Kids today are part of the most energy-intensive generation in history. They demand lots of electricity. And they deserve clean air."

A Dirty Industry

In reality, not only are vast amounts of fossil fuels burned to mine and refine the uranium for nuclear power reactors, polluting the atmosphere, but those plants are allowed "to emit hundreds of curies of radioactive gases and other radioactive elements into the environment every year," Dr. Helen Caldicott, the antinuclear authority, points out in her book *Nuclear Power Is Not the Answer.*

Sherwood Ross, "Nuclear Power Not Clean, Green or Safe," OpEdNews.com, January 8, 2007. www.opednews.com. Reproduced by permission.

What's more, the thousands of tons of solid radioactive waste accumulating in the cooling pools next to those plants contain "extremely toxic elements that will inevitably pollute the environment and human food chains, a legacy that will lead to epidemics of cancer, leukemia, and genetic disease in populations living near nuclear power plants or radioactive waste facilities for many generations to come," she writes. Countless Americans are already dead or dying as a result of those nuclear plants, and that story is not being effectively told.

Countless Americans are already dead or dying as a result of . . . nuclear plants, and that story is not being effectively told.

To begin with, over half of the nation's dwindling uranium deposits lie under Navajo and Pueblo tribal lands, and at least one in five tribal members recruited to mine the ore were exposed to the radioactive gas radon-220 and "have died and are continuing to die of lung cancer," Caldicott writes. "Thousands of Navajos are still affected by uranium-induced cancers," she adds.

As for uranium tailings discarded in the extraction process, 265 million tons of it have been left to pile up in, and pollute, the Southwest, even though they contain radioactive thorium. At the same time, uranium-238, also known as "depleted uranium," (DU) a discarded nuclear plant by-product, "is lying around in thousands of leaking, disintegrating barrels" at the enrichment facilities in Oak Ridge, Tenn.; Portsmouth, Ohio; and Paducah, Ky., where groundwater is now too polluted to drink, Caldicott writes.

Fuel rods at every nuclear plant leak radioactive gases or are routinely vented into the atmosphere by plant operators.

"Although the nuclear industry claims it is 'emission free,' in fact it is collectively releasing millions of curies annually," the author notes.

Safety Concerns

Speaking of safety, since the Three Mile Island (TMI) plant meltdown on March 28, 1979, some 2,000 Harrisburg area residents settled sickness claims with operators' General Public Utilities Corp. and Metropolitan Edison Co., the owners of TMI.

Area residents' symptoms included nausea, vomiting, diarrhea, bleeding from the nose, a metallic taste in the mouth, hair loss, and red skin rash, typical of acute radiation sickness when people are exposed to whole-body doses of radiation around 100 rads [a unit of absorbed radiation], said Caldicott, who arrived on the scene a week after the meltdown.

David Lochbaum, of the Union of Concerned Scientists, believes nuclear plant safety standards are lacking and predicted another nuclear catastrophe in the near future, stating, "It's not if, but when." Not only are such plants unsafe, but the spent fuel is often hauled long distances through cities to waste storage facilities where it will have to be guarded for an estimated 240,000 years.

[Three Mile Island] area residents' symptoms [were] typical of acute radiation sickness when people are exposed to whole-body doses of radiation around 100 rads.

"The magnitude of the radiation generated in a nuclear power plant is almost beyond belief," Caldicott writes. "The original uranium fuel that is subject to the fission process becomes 1 billion times more radioactive in the reactor core. A thousand-megawatt nuclear power plant contains as much long-lived radiation as that produced by the explosion of 1,000 Hiroshima-sized bombs."

Each year, operators must remove a third of the radioactive fuel rods from their reactors as they have become contaminated with fission products. The rods are so hot they must be stored for 30 to 60 years in a heavily shielded building continuously cooled by air or water lest they burst into flames, and afterwards packed into a container.

"Construction of these highly specialized containers uses as much energy as construction of the original reactor itself, which is 80 gigajoules per metric ton," Caldicott points out.

What's a big construction project, though, when you don't have to pay for it? In the 2005 energy bill, Congress allocated $13 billion in subsidies to the nuclear power industry. Between 1948 and 1998, the U.S. government subsidized the industry with $70 billion of taxpayer monies for research and development, corporate socialism, pure and simple.

As for safety, an accident or terrorist strike at a nuclear facility could kill people by the thousands. About 17 million people live within a 50-mile radius of the two Indian Point reactors in Buchanan, N.Y., just 35 miles from Manhattan. Suicidal terrorists, Caldicott noted, could disrupt the plant's electricity supply by ramming a speedboat packed with explosives into their Hudson River intake pipes, where water is sucked in to cool the reactors. Over time, the subsequent meltdown could claim an estimated 518,000 lives.

Caldicott points out there are truly green and clean alternative energy sources to nuclear power. She refers to the American plains as "the Saudi Arabia of wind," where readily available rural land in just several Dakota counties "could produce twice the amount of electricity that the United States currently consumes." Now that sounds clean, green, and safe. And I betcha it could be done through free enterprise, too. Somebody, quick, call in the entrepreneurs!

CHAPTER 3

Is Nuclear Energy a Good Solution to Climate Change?

Chapter Preface

Many nations are now deciding what role nuclear energy should play in their energy future, but one country—France—has already embraced nuclear power as its main source of electrical production. France invested in nuclear energy several decades ago and currently obtains more than 75 percent of its electricity from fifty-nine nuclear reactors situated throughout the country. France also has developed the ability to reprocess its nuclear fuel, and it is a leader in advanced nuclear technology. Once an electricity importer, France now is a major exporter, and electricity ranks as the country's fourth largest export. In addition, its electricity costs are among the lowest in Europe. Most observers agree that the French nuclear program has been a great scientific, engineering, and political success.

The French made the decision to greatly expand the country's nuclear energy capacity in 1974, following an oil crisis that began in October 1973. The crisis resulted in an Arab oil embargo when Arab members of the Organization of Arab Petroleum Exporting Countries (OAPEC), plus Egypt and Syria, decided to cut off shipments of oil to the United States and other countries who supported Israel during the 1973 Arab-Israeli war. The embargo quadrupled the price of oil, shook the world economy, and lasted until March 1974. The embargo caused some oil-dependent countries to reevaluate their energy policies and their dependence on foreign oil. The French government made this calculation and decided to scale up its investment in nuclear energy, largely because nuclear requires only a small amount of imported uranium fuel.

France's success in the nuclear field has been attributed to several key policy decisions. First, the French government strongly and consistently backed the program over many years, helping to finance much of the development costs for EDF,

France's nuclear utility company. Also, France was able to attract and train an elite, highly educated corps of technocrats to develop and run its nuclear plants and conduct necessary research. Another important decision was to standardize reactor types, choosing pressurized water reactors (PWRs), which are very durable and have few maintenance problems. All but one of the French nuclear plants use PWRs designed by the company Framatome, which is now called AREVA NP. This standardization has helped to reduce the costs of building, maintaining, and running reactors and has cut the cost of generating electricity. Finally, France opted to reprocess—that is, recycle—its spent uranium fuel to minimize the amount of radioactive waste from nuclear power plants.

The French nuclear program does have its critics, however. Antinuclear advocates continue to point out the drawbacks of using nuclear power, including safety and security concerns. In 2008, an accident at one of France's nuclear power plants caused uranium solution to be released into nearby rivers, and shortly thereafter, a pipe leak exposed one hundred workers to low doses of radiation. Another problem as yet unsolved is where to put the radioactive waste; reprocessing reduces the amount of waste, but does not eliminate it. In addition, most of the country's nuclear plants are located inland, many on rivers, where they use massive amounts of fresh water for cooling the reactors. Government regulations on the temperature of water discharged from nuclear plants often limits plant production, as does drought, which reduces the ability of rivers to disperse the heated water from plants. In the summer of 2009, a water crisis in France forced the shutdown of one-third of the country's nuclear power plants. Critics also suggest that the availability of cheaper electricity encourages people to use more power than they would otherwise. In any case, nuclear power only accounts for about 16 percent of total energy use; the French population continues to use fossil fuels for transportation and other purposes. In 2006, for example, 70 percent of the country's total energy consumption was from fossil fuels.

Despite these problems, the French population appears to accept the use of nuclear energy more than people in other countries, such as the United States. Commentators have suggested a number of reasons for this pronuclear attitude. Some credit the French government with doing a good job of promoting the positive aspects of nuclear energy, especially the idea of energy independence, which appeals to the independent-minded French. In addition, France has a long tradition of valuing scientists and engineers and supporting large technological projects, such as high-speed trains. The nuclear program, too, has brought jobs and prosperity to many French towns, helping to convince local residents that the positives of nuclear energy outweigh the negatives.

The threat of climate change has helped to ensure that nuclear energy will likely remain a large part of France's energy mix, and other countries considering nuclear programs as part of their global warming strategy are studying the French example. The authors of viewpoints in this chapter debate the issue of whether nuclear energy is truly a good solution to climate change.

Only Nuclear Can Provide All the Green Energy We Need

Max Schulz

Max Schulz is a senior fellow at the Manhattan Institute for Policy Research, a public policy organization that publishes City Journal, *a quarterly magazine about culture, domestic policy, urban affairs, and civic life.*

Exactly 30 years ago this Saturday [March 28, 2009], a stuck cooling valve and faulty control room instruments at Three Mile Island caused a partial meltdown of the core of one of the site's two nuclear reactors. The accident didn't kill or even harm anyone. Yet the U.S. nuclear industry continues to pay an enormous price three decades later. It's time to acknowledge—and embrace—the realities of nuclear power. In an age of increasing worries about climate change, nuclear power is the only technology capable of generating the large volumes of power our economy requires while emitting no pollution or greenhouse gases. And it does so safely, contrary to the hysterical reports that have dogged the nuclear industry since the accident.

Better than Solar or Wind Energy

In the wake of the Three Mile Island accident—and partly because of the strong antinuclear sentiment it generated—utilities canceled as many as 64 planned nuclear reactor units at various stages in the permitting and construction process. The industry ground to a virtual halt: We haven't seen a single nuclear plant proposed, licensed, and constructed in the intervening years.

Max Schulz, "Three Mile Island's Three-Decade Mark: It's Time to End the Nuclear Industry's 30-Year Sentence," *City Journal*, March 26, 2009. Reproduced by permission.

117

The environmentalists who helped thwart nuclear power after the accident, and who now agitate for "green" energy sources like wind turbines and solar power, would be wise to consider a few numbers. Those 64 planned nuclear reactors would have been capable of generating more than 500 billion kilowatt-hours of electricity annually, which would have helped avoid about 465 million metric tons of carbon dioxide emissions, putting us well on the way to meeting the emissions reductions goals under the Kyoto Protocol that [former president] Bill Clinton signed. No offense to wind and solar [power], but they simply aren't in the same league. Today's typical commercial nuclear reactor generates 1,000 megawatts of electricity and occupies perhaps 250 acres. To get the same amount of energy from wind would require 60,000 acres of 50-story-high wind turbines. The equivalent solar farm would need 11,000 acres. And even then, these technologies can't generate power around the clock—as nuclear can—because, well, the wind doesn't always blow and the sun doesn't always shine.

Nuclear power is the only technology capable of generating the large volumes of power our economy requires while emitting no pollution or greenhouse gases. And it does so safely.

A Safe Industry

Nuclear power is safe, too. The realization after the accident that, as one executive of the industry's trade group puts it, "with nuclear energy, an accident anywhere is an accident everywhere," prompted a thorough overhauling of how nuclear plants were run and a renewed commitment to safety. The 40 licensed operators currently at Three Mile Island's remaining reactor, for example, spend one week out of every six in training, and they're routinely retested according to the NRC [U.S.

Nuclear Regulatory Commission] regulations. The result has been unqualified success in terms of safety and efficiency at the plant. Its operators boast of having set four separate world records for continuous days of operation.

Public opinion has shifted considerably in favor of nuclear power in recent years. A new Gallup poll finds that 59 percent of Americans support nuclear power, 27 percent "strongly." That sentiment is reflected in the cautious optimism of utilities expressing interest in building new reactors. The NRC has fielded license applications to build more than two dozen new reactors in the coming years. If all are built, the nuclear industry predicts the creation of 100,000 additional jobs—"green" jobs not dependent on government stimulus.

Thirty years is a long time, especially in an era of technological breakthroughs. The Three Mile Island accident took place at a time of bell bottoms, Studio 54, and wonderment over things like pocket calculators and cassette recorders. Like most technologies, nuclear power has improved substantially since then. It's time to end the nuclear industry's long captivity—and start building new reactors.

Nuclear Is America's Best Hope for Affordable Green Energy

Lamar Alexander

Lamar Alexander is a Republican senator from Tennessee and conference chair of the Republican Party.

With the Waxman-Markey climate change and energy bill (American Clean Energy and Security Act) now [July 2009] passed by the House of Representatives and moving to the Senate, we need to take a moment to reflect on exactly what it is we are trying to accomplish with this legislation.

Proposed Climate Bill— The Wrong Direction

What kind of America do we hope to create in the next 20 years?

- We want an America in which we have enough clean, cheap, and reliable energy to create good jobs and run a prosperous industrial and high-tech society. In order to support the American economy that creates about 25 percent of the world's wealth, we need to produce about 25 percent of the world's energy.

- We want an America in which we are not creating excessive carbon emissions and running the risk of encouraging global warming.

- We want an America with cleaner air—where smog in Los Angeles and in the Great Smoky Mountains is a

Lamar Alexander, "Blueprint for 100 Nuclear Power Plants in 20 Years," U.S. Senate Republican Conference, July 13, 2009.

thing of the past—and where our children are less likely to suffer asthma attacks brought on by breathing pollutants.

• We want an America in which we are not creating "energy sprawl" by occupying vast tracts of farmlands, deserts, and mountaintops with energy installations that ruin scenic landscapes. The great American outdoors is a revered part of the American character. We have spent a century preserving it. We do not want to destroy the environment in the name of saving the environment.

• We want an America in which we create hundreds of thousands of "green jobs" but not at the expense of destroying tens of millions of red, white, and blue jobs. It doesn't make any sense to employ people in the renewable energy sector if we are throwing them out of work in manufacturing and high-tech. That's what will happen if these new technologies raise the price of electricity and send manufacturing and other energy-intensive industries overseas searching for cheap energy. We want new, clean, energy-efficient cars, but we want them built in Michigan, Ohio, and Tennessee, not Japan and Mexico.

• We want an America where we are the unquestioned champion in cutting-edge scientific research and lead the world in creating the new technologies of the future.

• And we want an America capable of producing enough of our own energy so that we can't be held hostage by some other energy-producing country.

None of these goals are met by the Waxman-Markey Bill. What started out as an effort to address global warming by reducing carbon emissions has ended up as a huge and unnecessary burden on the economy, a $100 billion a year job-killing national energy tax that will create a new utility bill for every American family.

Nuclear is already our best source for large amounts of cheap, reliable, and clean energy.

This tax burden is relieved only by the vague hope that all this can be overcome by mandating increased use of a few alternative energy sources defined as "renewable." Renewable energies such as wind, solar, and biomass are intriguing and promising as a supplement to America's energy requirements. Yet the Waxman-Markey Bill proves once again that one of government's biggest mistakes is taking a good idea and expanding it until it doesn't work anymore.

Trying to expand these forms of renewable energy to the point where they become our prime source of energy has huge costs and obvious flaws that may be impossible to overcome. What's worse, such an effort in renewable energy creates a whole new problem—"energy sprawl"—where we are asked to sacrifice the American landscape and overwhelm fragile ecosystems with thousands of massive energy machines in an effort to take care of our energy needs.

Is this really the America we want?

Nuclear Is a Better Option

There's a better option. Let's take another long, hard look at nuclear power. Nuclear is already our best source for large amounts of cheap, reliable, and clean energy. It provides only 20 percent of our nation's electricity but 70 percent of our carbon-free, pollution-free electricity. It is already far and away our best defense against global warming.

So why not build 100 new nuclear power plants during the next 20 years? American utilities built 100 reactors between 1970 and 1990 with their own (ratepayers') money.

Why can't we do it again? Other countries are already forging ahead of us. France gets 80 percent of its electricity from 50 reactors and has among the cheapest electricity rates and the lowest carbon emissions in Europe to show for it.

Japan is building reactors from start to finish in four years. China is planning 60 new reactors while Russia is selling its nuclear technology all over the world. India is making plans. President [Barack] Obama has even said Iran has the right to use nuclear power for energy. We invented this technology. Isn't it time we got back in the game?

One hundred new [nuclear] plants in 20 years would double U.S. nuclear production, making it about 40 percent of all electricity production.

There seem to be two things holding us back:

1. An exaggerated fear of nuclear technology.
2. A failure to appreciate just how different nuclear is from other technologies—how its tremendous energy density translates into a vanishingly small environmental footprint. . . .

A Clean Energy Policy

Nuclear power is the obvious first step to a policy of clean but low-cost energy. One hundred new plants in 20 years would double U.S. nuclear production, making it about 40 percent of all electricity production. Add 10 percent for sun and wind and other renewables, another 10 percent for hydroelectric and maybe 5 percent more natural gas—and we begin to have a cheap as well as clean energy policy.

Step two for a cheap and clean energy policy is to electrify half our cars and trucks. There is so much unused electricity at night that we could do this right now without building one new power plant, if we plug in vehicles while we sleep. Of course, that would increase our coal usage, which is why we also need more nuclear power. This is the fastest way to reduce dependence on foreign oil, keep fuel prices low, and reduce the one-third of the carbon dioxide that comes from gasoline engines.

Step three is to explore offshore for natural gas (it's low-carbon compared to coal) and oil (using less, but using our own).

The difficulties with nuclear power are political not technological, social not economic.

The final step is to double funding for energy research and development and launch several mini–Manhattan Projects like the one we had in World War II; this time to meet seven grand-energy challenges: improving batteries for plug-in vehicles, making solar power cost competitive with fossil fuels, making carbon capture a reality for coal burning plants, safely recycling used nuclear fuel, making advanced biofuels (from crops we don't eat) cost-competitive with gasoline, making more buildings green buildings and providing energy from fusion.

The difficulties with nuclear power are political not technological, social not economic. The main obstacle is a lingering doubt and fear in the public mind about the technology. Any progressive administration that wishes to solve the problem of global warming without crushing the American economy should help the public resolve these doubts and fears. What is needed boils down to two words: presidential leadership.

We can't wait any longer to start building our future of clean, reliable and affordable energy. The time has come for action. We can revive America's industrial and high-tech economy with the technology we already have at hand. The only requirement is that we open our minds to the possibilities and potential of nuclear power.

As we do, our policy of cheap and clean energy based upon nuclear power, electric cars, offshore exploration, and doubling energy R&D [research and development] will relieve strained family budgets and a sick economy with 10 percent unemployment. It will also prove to be the fastest way to increase American energy independence, clean the air, and reduce global warming.

We Must Consider Nuclear Energy as Part of Our Climate Change Solution

Eileen Claussen

Eileen Claussen is president of the Pew Center on Global Climate Change, a nonprofit advocacy group that conducts research on climate change worldwide.

Over the last decade, the case for a skeptical, wait-and-see approach to climate change has melted faster than summer sea ice in the Arctic. We now know from the science that this is a real and urgent problem. The most recent report from the Intergovernmental Panel on Climate Change [IPCC] projected that global temperatures will increase between 3.2 and 7.2 degrees Fahrenheit by 2100. Sea levels will rise by as much as a foot to a foot-and-a-half. Many species will be lost. In addition, there is a 90 percent chance or greater that the world will see more hot extremes, heat waves and heavy precipitation events. And it is likely we will see more droughts as well.

And this is not solely a problem of the future; it is happening right now. I mentioned the Arctic sea ice. This summer [2007], we saw it shrink to its smallest recorded extent ever. According to the National Snow and Ice Data Center, at the height of the melting, sea ice declined at a rate of 81,000 square miles per day. That's the equivalent of losing an area the size of Kansas—in a day. Researchers say this rate of loss was unprecedented in the satellite record. Of course, the sea ice will come back as winter temperatures return, but even the wintertime ice has been in decline—with 2007 and 2006 marking the lowest winter ice extent ever.

Eileen Claussen, "Reality Before the Renaissance: Making Nuclear Power Part of the Climate Solution," Speech at the American Nuclear Society/European Nuclear Society International Meeting, Washington, DC, November 12, 2007. Reproduced by permission.

Clearly, we have a very serious problem on our hands. And the reason we know we have a problem is because of the science, which now tells us in unequivocal terms that, if left unabated, climate change will have tremendous negative consequences for our country and our world.

The science also tells us something else. . . . It tells us there is no longer any doubt about what is causing this problem: greenhouse gas emissions from human sources—and, most of those emissions come from three key sectors: electricity; transportation, primarily automobiles; and buildings.

Dramatic Changes Necessary

As a result of all these emissions, the level of greenhouse gases in our atmosphere is growing. Advance details from the latest IPCC synthesis report tell us we are at 450 parts per million already; that is a measure of CO_2-equivalent greenhouse gases in the atmosphere, if we discount the shading effect of aerosols. And the reason why this number (450 parts per million) is significant is that we have reached this level more than a decade earlier than we thought just a short time ago. What's more, scientists tell us that in order to avoid the worst consequences of climate change, we must stabilize atmospheric concentrations of greenhouse gases at a level of roughly—you guessed it—450 parts per million. Obviously, this is a mammoth task that will require bold actions, actions that must begin now and continue for decades to come.

Nuclear is one of the few options on the table for producing electricity with no carbon emissions.

What kind of actions? Well, to stabilize greenhouse gases in the atmosphere at this level, we need to reduce worldwide emissions by 60 to 80 percent before 2050—60 to 80 percent. And we know which sector of the economy is the largest single source of these emissions. Electricity generation. In the United

States alone, power generation and heat together produce 42 percent of all carbon dioxide emissions. Globally, the figure is 41 percent.

Now obviously, there is no way to reduce those emissions to the levels we need to see without making some dramatic changes. Many of you are familiar, I am sure, with the work of Robert Socolow at Princeton. Well, Professor Socolow took a very reasoned look at what kinds of actions it will take to prevent the worst effects of climate change. He came up with the concept of what he called "stabilization wedges." These wedges show various actions we can take to stabilize carbon dioxide emissions at the current level of 7 gigatons per year. I should note that the projection under a business-as-usual scenario is for those emissions to rise to 14 gigatons over the next 50 years. So basically, we need to lop 7 gigatons off the business-as-usual path. And, conveniently, the professor came up with seven wedges that could conceivably get this done. Each would deliver a 1-gigaton reduction in projected emissions.

Here is an example of a wedge: putting 2 billion cars on the road at 60 miles per gallon instead of 30 miles per gallon. Or, in the electric power sector, implementing carbon capture and storage at 1,600 large coal plants; or building 1 million 2-megawatt wind turbines to displace coal power. And here's the wedge that should be of interest to this group: building 700 gigawatts of nuclear capacity to displace coal power. Do the math and you see this is twice the current global nuclear capacity. Obviously, a huge endeavor—but it gives you an idea of the level of action that is needed to address this enormous problem we are facing.

Climate change is such a serious problem that we cannot afford to take any option off the table.

Professor Socolow is not recommending any specific solution. He is not saying that these wedges he talks about are the exact paths we have to take. No, he is showing us the kinds of things we need to be talking about, the kinds of actions we need to consider. And, with these wedges now in mind, we can begin to weigh what's doable—and where we might be able to find the reductions we need.

The Role of Nuclear Power

And so, as we look at these wedges, and as we scan the horizon for opportunities to reduce emissions of these gases in a substantial way, we have to consider how . . . nuclear power can be a part of the solution. We would be foolish not to. Nuclear is one of the few options on the table for producing electricity with no carbon emissions. And, it is already delivering 20 percent or more of U.S. electricity, and more in other countries: 78 percent in France, 54 percent in Belgium, 39 percent in South Korea, and 30 percent in Japan. The IAEA [International Atomic Energy Agency] says nuclear accounts for 15 percent of electricity generation worldwide.

Some environmental groups feel that this industry poses as serious a threat to the world as climate change itself and should therefore be opposed at all costs. At the Pew Center, we don't feel this way. What we have always said is that climate change is such a serious problem that we cannot afford to take any option off the table. We simply cannot ignore the fact that nuclear power could make a substantial contribution to our efforts to reduce greenhouse gases.

However, there are other things we can't ignore. And these are the potential problems associated with the expanded use of nuclear power in this country and throughout the world. . . . [The European] Renaissance taught us about the rewards that come with rendering and understanding things as they are in the real world. And these are not just artistic or spiritual rewards I am talking about. The growth of this industry, its continued success, ultimately will depend on whether it follows the advice of Jim Collins, the best-selling author of *Good to Great*. "Confront the brutal facts," he tells us. And the brutal facts for nuclear power include the fact that we as a society still have not resolved a number of threshold issues that are essential to this industry's future.

[The nuclear energy industry needs] to show the world that it can enjoy the benefits of nuclear power without creating new risks or imposing new burdens on societies and the environment.

Of course, nuclear power is not alone in this respect. Other energy technologies that could potentially deliver substantial reductions in emissions face their own hurdles. A lot of people, for example, myself included, regularly talk about how important it is that we figure out how to capture and sequester carbon emissions from coal-fired power plants, and do this on a large scale. But the technologies for doing this are still untested on a commercial scale at coal-fired power plants, we still haven't proven you can store these emissions underground over long periods of time, and there will likely be serious public concerns about injecting these gases into the earth.

Wind and solar power face obstacles, too. To get renewables to a level where they could make an appreciable difference in reducing emissions, we would have to deal with a whole host of issues—from public opposition to large-scale wind farms to the thorny problem of these energy sources being intermittent. We need large-scale electricity storage.

So yes, nuclear power is not alone in having its challenges. But to move ahead without a full accounting of those challenges, and without plans for addressing them in a serious way, is to doom this industry's renaissance before it even starts.

In other words, simply offering up a carbon-free source of electrical power is not enough. You need to do more. You need to show the world that it can enjoy the benefits of nuclear power without creating new risks or imposing new burdens on societies and the environment. The biggest brutal fact that this industry needs to confront? How to deal with nuclear waste.

Problems with Nuclear Power

We need a new conversation in this country, and around the world, about nuclear waste. This conversation should be founded on a cool-headed assessment of what is feasible and practical for us to do. Even if the Yucca Mountain site [in Nevada] ultimately is approved for long-term storage (and that's still a big "if"), it will be decades before any waste ends up in Nevada. That is a fact. Yes, we can continue to store waste at the plants where it's generated. But that's not a realistic strategy for the long haul, especially if we want to add capacity, which will only mean more places in more parts of the country where more and more of this waste is stored.

Transparency is crucial—[nuclear energy] companies need to build trust with the public so that people know [the companies] have taken every precaution.

We really need both an interim solution and a long-term solution. And it is time for a more serious conversation in this country about interim solutions for storing nuclear waste. I am talking, of course, about the potential of centralized dry cask storage, especially for spent fuel that currently is kept at decommissioned plants. Today, the debate is all about temporary vs. permanent storage. And it is getting us nowhere. It's like [Sean] Hannity and [Alan] Colmes. There is never any resolution. We need to resolve this issue. And, I believe we will have a better chance of resolving it if we begin a new conversation, if we ratchet down the rhetoric, and if we consider other options, such as interim storage in selected, centralized locations, while at the same time working to make long-term storage a reality.

Responding to the nuclear waste issue in a reasoned and responsible way also can yield progress against other obstacles to this industry's expansion. One of these obstacles is concern about reprocessing and nuclear proliferation.

Just the other week, we learned how the National Academy of Sciences [NAS] feels about the [George W.] Bush administration's signature waste-reprocessing plan. The Global Nuclear Energy Partnership—and I quote—"should not go forward," according to the NAS. Among the problems: It's too expensive and it's founded on unproven technologies.

It is hard to ignore the fact that more nuclear power means more waste and more reprocessing. While safeguards exist in the United States and other countries to prevent the spread of these materials, there remain real risks that would have to be addressed; and the ability to cope with these risks varies widely around the world.

There needs to be a price on carbon. That is the only way to create a level playing field for nuclear power.

Of course, these are not the only barriers to the expansion of nuclear power. There also continue to be public concerns about the safety of this industry. We all know that U.S. plants are safer and more secure than in the past. But this is a fight you will have to continue to fight. There is no way around it if you are going to be building more plants. Transparency is crucial—companies need to build trust with the public so that people know you have taken every precaution. And, as an industry, you also need to pay attention to what is happening in other countries. Expanding the use of nuclear power in places with weak regulatory oversight, or unproven construction practices, is not in the long-term interests of this industry. Because, as you all know very well, just one problem at one nuclear power facility anywhere in the world can be a problem for nuclear power everywhere.

The Issue of Cost

Last but not least among the potential barriers to nuclear power is the issue of cost. The participants in the Keystone Center discussions said a reasonable estimate for life cycle costs of nuclear power is between 8 and 11 cents per kilowatt-hour. Granted, this is higher than some industry and U.S. DOE [Department of Energy] estimates of 4 to 7 cents per kilowatt-hour, but there is no denying that nuclear power, under present-day circumstances, is expensive relative to its main competitor: coal. For comparison's sake, a coal plant operating without carbon capture has life cycle costs of around 4.8 cents per kilowatt-hour. A conventional coal-fired plant, in other words, produces electricity at roughly half the cost of a nuclear plant. This is a huge barrier to this industry's expansion, as all of you know very well.

But something interesting happens when you try to reduce greenhouse gas emissions from the coal-fired plant by adding carbon capture and sequestration. The life cycle cost goes up significantly, and according to estimates, could be as high as 8 cents, which is the same as the Keystone Center's low-end estimate for nuclear. So now, you start to reach a level of parity with coal. But again, this only happens if we launch a determined effort to capture carbon emissions from coal-fired plants.

And so even if we finally figure out solutions to the big issues like nuclear waste storage, this industry's competitiveness ultimately will depend on one question: whether the United States and the world finally get serious about reducing emissions of greenhouse gases. There needs to be a price on carbon. That is the only way to create a level playing field for nuclear power. And it is the only way, in the Pew Center's opinion, to achieve real progress in protecting the climate. . . .

USCAP [United States Climate Action Partnership, a group of businesses working for climate change legislation] believes Congress should pass legislation that sets firm short- and medium-term binding emissions targets in the United States. The ultimate goal: Reduce emissions by 60 to 80 percent by 2050. In the view of the USCAP partners, a cap-and-trade system should be the cornerstone of U.S. climate policy. Right now, the cap-and-trade legislation that's getting the most attention is the bill introduced by Senators Joe Lieberman and John Warner. And I believe very strongly that the nuclear power industry can and must play a constructive role in the debate on this measure.

The only caution I will offer is this: You need to focus on the big picture in this debate. And that is the competitive advantage this industry gains from a comprehensive climate policy that once and for all puts a price on carbon. More nuclear subsidies are not the answer; they are short-term, ephemeral, and they may well scuttle the chances for this bill (and others) by emboldening (or simply ticking off) your opponents.

Right now, the best subsidy for nuclear power is a comprehensive climate policy. Because the sooner we have a cap-and-trade program in place, the sooner we will be able to determine in a reasoned way which energy options make the most sense, both for the economy and for the environment. And the sooner this industry can get past the cost issue and have a real discussion about the potential of expanded nuclear power as a solution to our energy and environmental needs.

Nuclear Power Cannot Solve Climate Change

Sharon Squassoni

Sharon Squassoni is a senior associate with the Carnegie Endowment for International Peace, a private, nonprofit organization dedicated to advancing cooperation between nations and promoting active international engagement by the United States.

After several decades of disappointing growth, nuclear energy seems poised for a comeback. Talk of a "nuclear renaissance" includes perhaps a doubling or tripling of nuclear capacity by 2050, spreading nuclear power to new markets in the Middle East and Southeast Asia, and developing new kinds of reactors and fuel-reprocessing techniques. During the George W. Bush administration, the United States has promoted nuclear energy both at home and abroad. Programs like the 2006 Global Nuclear Energy Partnership and President Bush's 2007 joint declaration with then–Russian president Vladimir Putin to facilitate and support nuclear energy in developing countries have helped to promote the notion of a major worldwide nuclear revival.

But the reality of nuclear energy's future is more complicated. Projections for growth assume that government support will compensate for nuclear power's market liabilities and that perennial issues such as waste, safety, and proliferation will not be serious hurdles. However, without major changes in government policies and aggressive financial support, nuclear power is actually likely to account for a *declining* percentage of global electricity generation. For example, the International Energy Agency's *World Energy Outlook 2007* projects that with-

Sharon Squassoni, "Nuclear Renaissance: Is It Coming? Should It?" Carnegie Endowment for International Peace, Washington, DC, October 2008. www.carnegieendowment .org. Reprinted by permission of the publisher.

out policy changes, nuclear power's share of worldwide electricity generation will drop from 15 percent in 2007 to 9 percent in 2030.

Given the seriousness of these uncertainties, a sound post-Bush foreign—and domestic—policy on nuclear energy should be based not on hope but on solid answers to six questions:

- Can nuclear power significantly enhance energy security?

- Can nuclear power contribute significantly to needed reductions in carbon emissions?

- Is nuclear power economically competitive?

- Can safety be assured for a greatly expanded number of nuclear reactors and associated facilities?

- Is an acceptable solution for nuclear waste in place or soon to be available?

- Can nuclear power be expanded in such a way as to adequately control the added risks of proliferation?

Can Nuclear Power Enhance Energy Security?

Rising prices of oil and natural gas have had a cascading effect on countries' concerns about energy security. Price disputes have resulted in temporary cutoffs of natural gas supplies in Europe in the past few years. But most countries will not be able to reduce their dependence on foreign oil by building nuclear power plants. Nuclear power—because it currently only provides electricity—is inherently limited in its ability to reduce this dependence. In the United States, for example, 40 percent of the energy consumed comes from oil, yet oil produces only 1.6 percent of electricity. And even though France and Japan rely heavily on nuclear energy, they have been unable to reduce their dependence on foreign oil because of oil's importance for transportation and industry.

Worldwide, the picture is similar. Oil accounts for about 7 percent of power generation globally, a share that is expected to decline to 3 percent by 2030. Only in the Middle East, where countries rely on oil for about 30 percent of their electricity generation, could substitution of nuclear power for oil make a significant difference. Until transportation switches to electricity as its fuel, nuclear energy largely will not displace oil.

Nuclear power is not a near-term solution to the challenge of climate change.

The situation is different for natural gas. Although natural gas also has industrial and heating uses, it produces about one-fifth of electricity worldwide. Natural gas is attractive as a way to produce electricity because gas-fired generating plants are very efficient at converting primary energy into electricity and also cheap to build, compared with coal- and nuclear-fired plants. Nuclear energy could displace natural gas for electricity production and improve some countries' stability of energy supply.

Ultimately, however, countries may be trading one form of energy dependence for another. Given the structure of the nuclear industry and uranium resource distribution, most countries will need to import fuel, technology, and reactor components, as well as fuel services. This means that few countries can expect more than *interdependence*, even when it comes to nuclear power.

Can Nuclear Power Contribute to Controlling Climate Change?

Nuclear power is not a near-term solution to the challenge of climate change. The need to immediately and dramatically reduce carbon emissions calls for approaches that can be implemented more quickly than building nuclear reactors. It also calls for actions that span all energy applications, not just electricity. Improved efficiency in residential and commercial buildings, industry, and transport is the first choice among all options in virtually all analyses of the problem. Nuclear energy will remain an option among efforts to control climate change, but given the maximum rate at which new reactors can be built, much new construction will simply offset the retirement of nuclear reactors built decades ago.

For nuclear energy to make a larger difference in meeting the challenge of climate change, the industry would need to add capacity exceeding replacement levels. According to a 2007 study by the Keystone Center, this would require "the industry to return immediately to the most rapid period of growth experienced in the past (1981–1990) and sustain this rate of growth for 50 years." This would mean completing twenty-one to twenty-five new, large (1,000 megawatts electric) plants each year through 2050.

Yet the global nuclear construction industry has shrunk. In the past twenty years, there have been fewer than ten new reactor construction starts worldwide in any given year. Today there are already bottlenecks in the global supply chain, including ultra-heavy forgings, large manufactured components, engineering, craft labor, and skilled construction labor. All these constraints have been exacerbated by the lack of recent experience in building nuclear plants and by aging labor forces.

The current economic crisis could make financing nuclear power plants particularly difficult.

In addition to the major nuclear reactor vendors, supporting industries will also either need to be rebuilt or recertified to nuclear standards. In the United States, there has been a significant decline of supporting industries. In the 1980s, the United States had 400 nuclear suppliers and 900 holders of N-stamp certificates from the American Society of Mechanical Engineers. Today, there are just 80 suppliers and 200 N-stamp holders. In countries that have never had nuclear power plants, qualified subcontractors and labor would have to be trained and certified.

Will New Nuclear Power Plants Be Economically Competitive?

The economic competitiveness of nuclear power is a subject of much debate. Nuclear power plants are expensive to build but relatively inexpensive to operate, because their fuel costs are low compared with alternatives. For example, the price of natural gas accounts for 85 percent of the variable cost of a kilowatt-hour, whereas nuclear fuel accounts for 27 percent. This means that as the cost of fossil fuels rise, either due to short supply or because carbon dioxide emissions may in the future be regulated, nuclear power will become relatively more competitive. There is already evidence in the United States that coal plants may become increasingly difficult to build because of public awareness of their environmental impact. U.S. nuclear industry executives have suggested that a carbon-pricing framework would be necessary to provide incentives for utilities to build more than a handful of nuclear power plants.

A big uncertainty is the cost of constructing new nuclear power plants. As a general rule, about two-thirds of a nuclear reactor's cost stems from construction. Factors affecting this cost of construction include the creditworthiness of the companies involved in building the reactors, the cost of capital (especially debt) over the next decade, the risk of cost escalation due to construction delays and overruns, the need for additional generating capacity in a slowing economy, and the competitive advantage of both traditional and emerging power generation technologies.

Because data from the past unfortunately provide little help in assessing future costs, the real costs of new nuclear power plants may not be known for years. In fact, Moody's [Investors Service] stated in a special October 2007 report that "the ultimate costs associated with building new nuclear generation do not exist today—and that the current cost estimates represent best estimates, which are subject to change.". . .

The current economic crisis could make financing nuclear power plants particularly difficult. Financing costs account for between 25 and 80 percent of the total cost of construction because nuclear power plants take much longer to build than alternatives (for example, wind plants require eighteen months to build, combined-cycle gas turbines need thirty-six months, and nuclear power plants take at least sixty months). A global tightening of risk management standards in the wake of the current economic crisis could imperil the nuclear industry in particular, because a reactor entails such a large investment (between $5 billion and $10 billion per plant) relative to the typical financial resources of electric utilities.

More than fifty years since the first reactor produced electricity, no country has yet opened a permanent site for nuclear waste.

Thus, new nuclear power plants will almost certainly continue to be difficult to finance, particularly in the United States. In developing countries and other countries where public funding is likely, governments will need to assess whether nuclear energy is the least costly way to provide climate-friendly energy compared with possible alternatives.

Can Safety Be Assured?

Concerns about the safety of nuclear power plants have played a major role in nuclear power's stagnation over the past two decades. Newer designs are much simpler and have built-in passive safety measures. Yet a big expansion of nuclear power could lead to new safety concerns. New suppliers from South Korea, China, and India could enter the field to meet expanded demand, and there is some evidence that Chinese subcontractors for U.S. reactors in China have not met some quality control standards.

In addition, countries that are new to nuclear power must not only implement a complex set of regulations and laws, but also foster the development of resilient safety and security cultures. This could be quite challenging for some developing countries. Finally, in states with existing power plants, the extension of reactor operations beyond their initial lives of thirty or forty years to sixty or even eighty years could potentially result in new safety concerns if construction materials age in unanticipated ways.

Is an Acceptable Solution to Nuclear Waste at Hand?

Nuclear reactors unavoidably generate radioactive spent fuel as waste. Some states will opt to store spent nuclear fuel indefinitely. Others may seek to recycle it, using a technique known as reprocessing, which reduces the volume of waste that needs to be stored but produces separated plutonium, a nuclear weapons fuel. More than fifty years since the first reactor produced electricity, no country has yet opened a permanent site for nuclear waste (known as a geologic repository). Such a repository is still needed, even if the recycling route is taken, because there have been significant technical and, more important, political hurdles in finding appropriate sites.

Whether nations are storing spent fuel or recycled waste, adequate physical protection and security against terrorist access are both essential. Even in fuel-leasing schemes, in which spent fuel would be shipped back to the original supplier, new nuclear states will still require safe and secure interim storage for fuel as it cools.

A key question for the future of nuclear energy is how many countries will choose to reprocess their fuel. Some states, such as South Korea, are interested in reprocessing to reduce the volume of their spent fuel. Japan has been reprocessing its spent fuel to both reduce the volume and use the plutonium for fuel as part of an effort to strengthen its energy security. Although there is much evidence that the use of mixed fuel (plutonium and uranium) in reactors is uneconomical, some countries may use it anyway. This would vastly increase the quantities of nuclear weapons material available around the world. . . .

Only nuclear energy . . . requires international inspections to ensure that material, equipment, facilities, and expertise are not misused for weapons purposes.

Can Proliferation Risks Be Adequately Controlled?

More than twenty-five states . . . have newly expressed interest in nuclear power. Some of these countries have more detailed plans than others, but the International Atomic Energy Agency (IAEA) has cautioned that states just beginning to embark on the path toward nuclear energy can expect at least fifteen years to elapse before their first plant begins operation. They will need this time to develop the necessary physical and intellectual infrastructures to run nuclear power plants safely and securely.

Many of the countries interested in nuclear power anticipate sizable growth in electricity demand. Others may simply be jumping on the nuclear bandwagon, either to make a national statement about capabilities or to take advantage of what they may perceive as incentives from advanced nuclear states, particularly France, Russia, and the United States. Recent official nuclear cooperation agreements—between France and Algeria, Libya, Morocco, and the United Arab Emirates; between the United States and India, Jordan, Turkey, and, potentially, Bahrain; and between Russia and Algeria, Armenia, Myanmar, Venezuela, and Vietnam—have contributed to the increasingly widespread perception that nuclear power is attractive.

In 2008, the International Security Advisory Board of the U.S. Department of State concluded that "the rise in nuclear power worldwide, and particularly within third world countries, inevitably increases the risks of proliferation." Only nuclear energy, among all energy sources, requires international inspections to ensure that material, equipment, facilities, and expertise are not misused for weapons purposes. For those countries that do not already have nuclear programs, developing the scientific, engineering, and technical base required for nuclear power would in itself heighten their proliferation potential. Political instability in many cases is a more prominent concern than weapons intentions. For example, the Group of Eight states [France, Germany, Italy, Japan, the United Kingdom, the United States, Canada, and Russia] are concerned about Nigeria's plans to develop nuclear power because of Nigeria's history of political instability. The possibility of nuclear reactors in Yemen would raise similar concerns. Regional dynamics also play a role in increasing risks. Especially in the Middle East and Southeast Asia, some countries might worry about and respond to the possibility that one of their neighbors was developing a weapons program.

Bearing in mind the risks that nuclear expansion could pose, and the number of currently unanswerable questions, the U.S. administration needs to carefully consider its policy toward a rapid expansion of nuclear power.

Nuclear Energy Costs Could Hinder Climate Change Solutions

Union of Concerned Scientists

The Union of Concerned Scientists is a science-based nonprofit organization that works for a healthy environment and a safer world.

Nuclear power could play a role in reducing global warming emissions because reactors emit almost no carbon while they operate and can have low life cycle emissions. Partly for that reason, advocates are calling for a nationwide investment in at least 100 new nuclear reactors, backed by greatly expanded federal loan guarantees. However, the industry must resolve major economic, safety, security, and waste disposal challenges before new nuclear reactors could make a significant contribution to reducing carbon emissions.

The economics of nuclear power alone could be the most difficult hurdle to surmount. A new UCS [Union of Concerned Scientists] analysis, *Climate 2030: A National Blueprint for a Clean Energy Economy*, finds that the United States does not need to significantly expand its reliance on nuclear power to make dramatic cuts in power plant carbon emissions through 2030—and indeed that new nuclear reactors would largely be uneconomical.

That analysis shows that by significantly expanding the use of energy efficiency and low-cost and declining-cost renewable energy sources, consumers and businesses could reduce carbon emissions from power plants as much as 84 percent by 2030 while saving $1.6 trillion on their energy bills. And, under the Blueprint scenario, . . . because of their high cost, the

Union of Concerned Scientists, "Nuclear Power: A Resurgence We Can't Afford," August 2009. www.ucsusa.org. Reproduced by permission.

nation would not build more than four new nuclear reactors already spurred by existing loan guarantees from the Department of Energy (DOE) and other incentives.

The [nuclear] industry must resolve major economic, safety, security, and waste disposal challenges before new nuclear reactors [contribute to] . . . reducing carbon emissions.

A forced nuclear resurgence, in contrast, could make efforts to cut the nation's global warming emissions much more costly, given the rising projected costs of new nuclear reactors. A nuclear power resurgence that relies on new federal loan guarantees would also risk repeating costly bailouts of the industry financed by taxpayers and ratepayers twice before.

The Status of Nuclear Power Today

The United States now obtains about 20 percent of its electricity from 104 nuclear reactors. Thanks to better operating performance, the "capacity factor" of U.S. reactors—the amount of power reactors actually produce, compared with their rated capacity—rose from 56 percent in 1980 to nearly 92 percent in 2008. However, U.S. utilities have ordered no new nuclear plants since 1978, and canceled all plants ordered after 1973. Other countries have continued to build nuclear plants, but at a much slower rate than during the peak years of the 1970s and 1980s.

The U.S. Nuclear Regulatory Commission (NRC) is in the process of extending the licenses for most, if not all, U.S. reactors now operating, from their original 40 years to 60 years. The industry is currently expected to retire almost all these reactors between 2030 and 2050. The industry has begun discussing the potential for further license extensions, although no one has determined the technical and economic feasibility and the safety implications of such extensions.

Fourteen companies have submitted applications to the NRC to build and operate 26 new plants at 17 sites. However, some companies have already withdrawn several applications after announcing plant cancellations or design changes.

A forced nuclear resurgence . . . could make efforts to cut the nation's global warming emissions much more costly.

The applications reference five different plant designs, of which the NRC has certified only two. And one of those, the AP1000, has undergone significant design changes since it was certified. The NRC is not expected to approve any applications before late 2011. Thus, even optimistic estimates suggest that no new plants will come online before 2016—and probably later.

A Record of Cost Overruns

The cost of nuclear power is driven largely by the cost of building the reactors. The fuel and operating costs of existing nuclear reactors are usually lower than those of other conventional technologies for producing electricity, due to the fact that their large capital costs have been largely written down over the years due to market forces and regulatory actions. However, high construction costs—coupled with long construction periods and associated financing costs—have been and continue to be the economic Achilles' heel of the nuclear industry.

During the 1970s and 1980s, utilities' cost overruns in building nuclear power plants averaged more than 200 percent, as construction costs skyrocketed even as growth in demand for electricity slowed. The result was what a 1985 *Forbes* cover story called "the largest managerial disaster in business history, a disaster on a monumental scale." Utilities abandoned some 100 plants during construction—more than half of the planned nuclear fleet. Taxpayers and ratepayers reimbursed utilities for most of the more than $40 billion cost of these abandoned plants.

Meanwhile, the nuclear plants that utilities did complete usually led to significant rate increases in electricity bills. Ratepayers bore well over $200 billion (in today's dollars) in cost overruns for completed nuclear plants. In the 1990s, legislators and regulators also allowed utilities to recover most "stranded costs"—the difference between utilities' remaining investments in nuclear plants and the market value of those plants—as states issued billions of dollars in bonds backed by ratepayer charges to pay for utilities' above-market investments.

High construction costs . . . have been and continue to be the economic Achilles' heel of the nuclear industry.

The total cost to ratepayers, taxpayers, and shareholders stemming from cost overruns, canceled plants, and stranded costs exceeded $300 billion in today's dollars.

A Nuclear Resurgence at What Cost?

Reliably projecting the construction costs of new U.S. nuclear plants is impossible, because the nation has no recent experience to draw on. Experience with reactors now under construction in Europe, however—along with trends in the cost of commodities used to build the plants, and in overall construction costs during most of the past decade—show the same vulnerability to cost escalation that plagued the last generation. Four years after its 2005 groundbreaking, for example, the Olkiluoto plant in Finland is reportedly three years behind schedule, with cost overruns topping 50 percent. The project has encountered numerous quality problems, and the principals are in arbitration over responsibility for the cost overruns.

An analysis by Cambridge Energy Research Associates shows that construction costs have risen for all technologies used to generate electricity over the past decade—but most dramatically for nuclear plants.

As recently as 2002, the industry and the DOE were projecting costs of $2 billion–$3 billion per new nuclear plant. However, developers applying for DOE loan guarantees in October 2008 for 21 proposed nuclear plants estimated that their costs—including financing costs and expected increases in construction costs—would total $188 billion. That translates into an average of $9 billion per plant.

The industry estimate also represents an average cost of more than $6,700 per kilowatt. By mid-2009, however, Wall Street and other independent analysts had raised projections of "overnight" construction costs for nuclear plants to as high as $10,000 per kilowatt. And those overnight costs do not include financing costs or cost escalation during construction, which can raise the total price of a nuclear power plant by as much as 50 percent.

A recent analysis by economist Mark Cooper of the Institute for Energy and the Environment at Vermont Law School showed that this cost escalation is consistent with the pattern that occurred in the 1970s and 1980s with the previous generation of nuclear plants.

Charging Ratepayers for Plants Under Construction

Given such high costs, a new nuclear plant can lead to significant increases in the price of electricity, even before the plant goes online. For example, Progress Energy—a utility that is building two new reactors in Florida at an expected cost of at least $17 billion—has received regulatory approval to charge ratepayers for construction work in progress (CWIP). These charges have already raised customers' average utility bills by

10 percent—with additional increases scheduled each year—although the plants will not generate a single kilowatt of electricity for at least a decade.

CWIP is receiving greater attention today as utilities seek to shift the costs and risks of building new reactors to ratepayers. Several states now allow electric companies to include CWIP in their rate base, while others are considering it. By phasing in charges during construction, a power producer can reduce the rate hike that typically occurs when a new nuclear power plant begins to operate. However, regulators largely abandoned this practice in the 1980s when consumers ended up paying for nuclear reactors later canceled because of cost overruns.

Nuclear vs. Low-Carbon Competitors

Climate 2030: A National Blueprint for a Clean Energy Economy, the recent UCS report, provides strong evidence that new nuclear plants are not cost-competitive with other electricity sources, including energy efficiency and renewable energy. That report provides a peer-reviewed analysis of the costs and benefits of reducing U.S. global warming emissions by 26 percent below 2005 levels by 2020, and 56 percent by 2030. Such cuts would put the United States on a path to reduce those emissions by at least 80 percent by 2050—a drop many scientists deem necessary to avoid the most dangerous effects of climate change.

A new nuclear plant can lead to significant increases in the price of electricity, even before the plant goes online.

To perform this analysis, the UCS authors used a modified version of the Department of Energy's Energy Information Administration's National Energy Modeling System (NEMS). The model chose the combination of new power sources needed to maintain a reliable supply of electricity at the lowest cost through 2030 while also meeting the emissions targets. The model factored in the costs of building new transmission lines, integrating renewable energy technologies into the grid, and providing reserve power supplies.

The model found that—especially given the recent escalation in cost estimates—new nuclear plants are likely to be among the more expensive options for producing low-carbon electricity. And the model did not consider that the costs of nuclear power are likely to continue to escalate during construction, given the industry's history. Nor did it consider the potential for a number of emerging renewable technologies to become available and cost-competitive.

The model analyzed two policy scenarios for achieving the targeted cuts in carbon emissions. The first scenario—called the Blueprint case—relied on a cap-and-trade system for putting a price on carbon emissions, plus policy incentives and standards to encourage robust reliance on energy efficiency and development of renewable sources of electricity. That scenario reflected earlier analyses showing that such policies can cut energy bills for consumers and businesses, thus lowering the overall cost of reducing carbon emissions. Energy efficiency measures, in particular, cost only about three cents per kilowatt-hour saved—much less than the cost of producing a kilowatt-hour of electricity from any new low-carbon technology.

The second scenario—called the No Complementary Policies case—stripped out the policies promoting efficiency and renewable energy. That left a relatively simple cap-and-trade system, and allowed technologies to "compete" to provide cuts in those emissions at the lowest cost. Both scenarios assumed that government would recycle revenues from auctioning allowances to emit carbon back into the economy, but that government would not target those revenues to specific uses, such as energy efficiency and low-carbon technologies.

The model confirmed that the first scenario was the least expensive for consumers and businesses. Their net savings— beyond the costs of investing in efficiency and renewable energy—would total $1.6 trillion by 2030, compared with business as usual. And that scenario would enable the nation to reduce global warming emissions from power plants by 84 percent by 2030.

According to the model, new nuclear plants would not play a significant role in either scenario. In the Blueprint case, the nation would not build any new nuclear plants beyond four 1,100-megawatt reactors already in the pipeline, spurred by existing nuclear subsidies and loan guarantees. That is because energy efficiency and renewable sources would meet nearly all the nation's needs for electricity, and for cutting emissions from that sector.

New nuclear plants are likely to be among the more expensive options for producing low-carbon electricity.

In the No Complementary Policies case, the lack of policies promoting energy efficiency would push electricity demand much higher and require more electricity supply. However, even in that scenario, the model found that the nation would build only 12 new nuclear plants by 2030—for a total of 13,600 megawatts—because renewable sources of electricity, and power produced from natural gas, would still be more cost-effective than nuclear power. Under that scenario, net energy savings for consumers and businesses would total $600 billion through 2030—a trillion dollars less than if policies spurred even greater investment in energy efficiency and renewable energy.

Thus the *Climate 2030* analysis shows that, despite optimistic assumptions about the costs of nuclear plants, they are not the most economical approach to meeting ambitious goals for cutting carbon through 2030. What's more, the nation does not need new nuclear plants to meet those goals, especially if public policies spur the use of more cost-effective energy efficiency and renewable energy.

Nuclear Energy Is Not Green Energy

Energy Justice Network

Energy Justice Network is a national environmental advocacy group that seeks a complete phaseout of nuclear power, fossil fuels, large hydroelectric dams, and biomass/incineration within the next twenty years.

Nuclear power is an expensive, polluting, dangerous, racist, depletable, and now foreign source of energy. 80–90% of uranium used in the U.S. is imported from Canada, Australia, the former Soviet Union and Africa. At the current consumption rate, low-cost uranium reserves will be exhausted in about 50 years.

Uranium Mining

The nuclear chain begins with uranium mining, a polluting activity that devastates large areas. Uranium ore can contain as little as 500 grams recoverable uranium per million grams of earth. Enormous amounts of rock have to be dug up, crushed and chemically processed to extract the uranium.

The remaining wastes, still containing large amounts of radioactivity, remain at the mines. These "tailings" are often stored in a very poor condition, resulting in the contamination of surface [water] and groundwater.

Natural uranium contains two different forms, or isotopes: U-238 and U-235. U-235 is fissionable, which means its atoms can be split, releasing large amounts of heat. However, natural uranium consists of more than 99% U-238 and less than 1% U-235. To be used as a fuel, large amounts of U-238 must be removed to increase the proportion of U-235 to 3–5%.

Energy Justice Network, "Nuclear Power," December 16, 2008. www.energyjustice.net. Reproduced by permission.

Nuclear Weapons

Depleted uranium (DU) is the U-238 waste product that has been "depleted" of U-235. DU has been used to make armor-piercing bullets, tank shielding and more. When used in warfare, DU bursts into flames upon impact, spreading uranium dust into the environment. DU is radioactive for billions of years and hundreds of tons of it have contaminated Iraq, Afghanistan, Bosnia and testing locations like Vieques, Puerto Rico. It's the primary culprit in Gulf War syndrome and many other health problems.

While the nuclear reactors themselves release few greenhouse gases, the nuclear fuel cycle is a significant contributor [to global warming].

The same process used to make reactor fuel can be used to highly enrich uranium for nuclear bombs. This is why nuclear power programs have led to nuclear weapons programs in other countries.

Pollution in the Nuclear Fuel Cycle

Many steps are required to make uranium suitable for use in nuclear reactors. From mining to milling to conversion to enrichment to fuel fabrication, each step involves separate facilities throughout the U.S., poisoning communities with radioactive and chemical pollution (mostly in western and midwestern states).

Global Warming

While the nuclear reactors themselves release few greenhouse gases, the nuclear fuel cycle is a significant contributor. In 2001, 93% of the nation's reported emissions of CFC-114, a potent greenhouse gas, were released from the United States Enrichment Corporation, where uranium is enriched to make nuclear reactor fuel. These facilities are so energy intensive that some of the nation's dirty, old coal plants exist just to power the nuclear fuel facilities.

Reactors and Health Impacts

Nuclear reactors themselves have serious environmental and public health impacts. Radioactive air and water pollution is released through the routine operation of all nuclear reactors. A wide range of radioactive isotopes are released with varying radioactive and chemical properties—some toxic, some not, some more radioactive than others, some lasting minutes, some lasting billions of years.

Living near a nuclear facility increases your chances of dying from breast cancer. A nationwide survey of 268 counties within 50 miles of 51 nuclear reactors found breast cancer deaths in these "nuclear counties" to be 10 times the national rate from 1950 to 1989.

In the 7 years after the closure of 8 nuclear reactors, infant mortality rates (deaths to infants under 1 year of age) fell dramatically in downwind communities.

Living near a nuclear facility increases your chances of dying from breast cancer.

Strontium-90, a radioactive pollutant now released only from nuclear reactors, ends up in milk and bones, contributing to bone cancer and leukemia. Studies of Sr-90 in baby teeth found levels 30–50% higher in teeth of children living near reactors. Background levels are rising with continued use of nuclear reactors, rising to levels comparable to when atmospheric nuclear bomb tests contaminated the nation in the 1940s and '50s. Levels in the teeth of babies born in the late 1990s are about 50% higher than those born in the late 1980s.

Of the 7 areas examined so far in the baby tooth studies, the highest Sr-90 levels have been found in southeastern PA [Pennsylvania]—around the Limerick reactor.

Living near reactors is also correlated with increases in leukemia and childhood cancer.

Water Use: Harming Wildlife

Reactors require huge amounts of cooling water, which is why they're often located near rivers, lakes or oceans. Reactors with cooling towers or ponds can use 28–30 million gallons of water per day. The 48 reactors with once-through cooling systems use far more (up to 1.5 billion gallons per day). A typical two-unit reactor using once-through cooling takes in about a square mile of water, 14 feet deep, each day.

The initial devastation of marine life and ecosystems stems from the powerful intake of water into the nuclear reactor. Marine life, ranging from endangered sea turtles and manatees down to delicate fish larvae and microscopic planktonic organisms vital to the ocean ecosystem, is sucked irresistibly into the reactor cooling system. Some of these animals are killed when trapped against filters, grates, and other structures, or, in the case of air-breathing animals like turtles, seals, and manatees, they drown or suffocate.

[High-level nuclear] waste will be hazardous for millions of years. No technology exists to keep it isolated this long.

An equally huge volume of wastewater is discharged at temperatures up to 25 [degrees Fahrenheit] . . . hotter than the water into which it flows. Indigenous marine life suited to colder temperatures is eliminated or forced to move, disrupting delicately balanced ecosystems.

Waste

Radioactive wastes are produced continually in reactors. There are two basic types of nuclear waste: high-level nuclear waste (the used fuel rods) and "low-level radioactive waste" (everything else).

High-level nuclear waste (also called irradiated or "spent" fuel) is literally about 1 million times more radioactive than when the fuel rods were loaded into the reactor. This waste is so lethal that standing near it without shielding would kill you within minutes. This waste will be hazardous for millions of years. No technology exists to keep it isolated this long. Irradiated fuel rods are stored in storage pools inside reactor buildings, often several stories high, where they're highly vulnerable to aircraft attacks. If the water is drained from the pool, exposing the rods to open air, a meltdown would cause a massive release of radiation. Some utilities have begun storing this waste in dry casks on outdoor concrete pads in the backyard of the reactors, introducing separate storage, packaging and security problems.

A permanent "disposal" site planned for Yucca Mountain, Nevada, has many problems. It's far from where most waste is produced, requiring unprecedented numbers of shipments through 43 states, risking accidents and attacks. Yucca Mountain is on Native American lands and is too leaky to keep the waste dry. The site is amid active fault lines and is too small to store the amount of waste that would be generated by the time it opens (if it ever does). Currently, a site on native lands in Utah is proposed to store the waste "temporarily."

"Low-level" radioactive waste (LLRW) is defined as all other radioactive waste from reactors, regardless of radioactivity levels or health hazards. Large amounts of this waste have been dumped or burned. Six official LLRW dumps exist in the United States. All are leaking, contaminating groundwater.

Environmental Racism

Nuclear power disproportionately affects communities of color, from the mining of uranium on Native American and aboriginal lands, to the targeting of black and Hispanic communities for new uranium processing facilities to the targeting of black and Hispanic and Native American communities for "low-level" nuclear waste dumps. All sites proposed for "temporary" and permanent storage of high-level nuclear waste have been Native American lands.

Too Expensive

Nuclear power is the most expensive form of power and could not exist with massive subsidies, including the "Price-Anderson" law that places a cap on industry liability in the event of a nuclear accident.

Fusion

Fusion still produces nuclear waste, including tritium, a very dangerous, hard-to-contain air and water contaminant. Like fission, it would be very expensive and highly centralized. Despite massive research spending, it's still decades away from reality. The same money spent on clean solutions (conservation, efficiency, wind and solar) would do far more.

Nuclear Energy Creates Hazards and Fails to Address Climate Change

Greenpeace International

Greenpeace International is an international environmental advocacy group.

The potential of renewable energy is vast and far greater than that of nuclear power or climate-changing fossil fuels. With today's technology we can generate almost six times the current global energy demand.

Why listen to the nuclear industry, which time and time again has offered us false promises and lies? Why let it drag us backwards to the past and believe that nuclear power is needed to tackle climate change when we can look to the future, a clean future based on renewable energy sources; a future free of more radioactive waste and the nuclear proliferation nightmare that accompanies nuclear power?

The choice is not just about how to replace existing power plants. One-third of the world's population, some 2 billion people have no reliable access to energy supplies; this inequity cannot be relieved by the 1950s nuclear nightmare, but only by the efficient use of diverse and decentralized renewable energy systems.

A Dangerous Diversion

The promotion of nuclear power as the answer to climate change is a dangerous diversion from the real solutions: A massive uptake of renewable energy and the adoption of energy efficiency are the only effective ways to combat climate

Greenpeace International, "Climate Change—Nuclear Not the Answer," accessed October 28, 2009. www.greenpeace.org. Reproduced by permission.

change. They are available now; they are clean, cheap and have the added benefit of providing energy security.

Nuclear power belongs in the dustbin of history; It is a target for terrorists, and a source of nuclear weapons. The future can be nuclear free. Renewable energy is peaceful energy and it is available today.

While the nuclear industry's 1950s dream of clean energy that would be too cheap to meter lies in economic and environmental tatters, that same industry is now desperately trying to convince us that it is the solution to climate change. While the world is struggling to manage the vast mountains of radioactive waste, which have been produced over the last half-century, many in the finance industry dismiss it as 'too expensive to matter'.

The promotion of nuclear power as the answer to climate change is a dangerous diversion from the real solutions: a massive uptake of renewable energy and . . . energy efficiency.

It is sobering to remember that 21 years ago on April 26, the industry was brought to a standstill by the world's worst nuclear accident at Chernobyl; an accident, which emitted an unstoppable and deadly plume of radioactivity that travelled the world and the effects of which can still be measured today; an accident, which could be repeated by any one of the world's 400 or so nuclear reactors.

Nuclear power has not suddenly become safer or cleaner. The legacy of the nuclear waste remains unsolved and accidents happen across the world daily. However, the nuclear industry is using climate change as an excuse to save and even expand its ailing business. The industry has a history of broken promises and lies; lies, which continue with its claim to be the solution to climate change.

The environmental, social, security and proliferation problems that have always plagued the nuclear industry continue to do so, despite over half a century of attempts to find solutions. We should not be conned into accepting one environmental threat on the premise that it will avert another when a future free of both nuclear and dangerous climate change is possible through the speedy deployment and development of renewable energy technologies and energy efficiency.

With the use of existing technology, Japan achieves energy intensity one-seventh of that of China (that's seven times more energy service per unit of energy used). Organisation for Economic Co-operation and Development (OECD) nations could save 30% of energy, and developing nations up to 50%. Lighting an average European household uses only a third of the energy used for lighting in U.S. households.

The environmental, social, security and proliferation problems that have always plagued the nuclear industry continue to do so, despite over half a century of attempts to find solutions.

Sweden gets 29% of its total energy supply—51% of its electricity—from renewables (2001—EU [European Union] averages of 5.8% and 15.5% respectively).

Key Reasons Against Nuclear

The key reasons why the self-serving nuclear industry arguments about its role in helping to fight climate change are wrong.

- Nuclear energy is an expensive diversion from the task of developing and deploying renewable energy, energy efficiency and the more decentralized energy systems required for a low-carbon future.

- We can reduce carbon emissions much more cheaply and more effectively using renewable energy and energy efficiency measures.

- No proven solution exists for dealing with radioactive waste.

- Expanding nuclear power internationally would hugely increase the risks from terrorism and nuclear weapons proliferation.

- Nuclear power plants cannot be built in time to make even the smallest difference.

Replacing Global Warming with a Nuclear Winter Is Not the Answer

The Massachusetts Institute of Technology (MIT) and other studies estimate that for nuclear power to have any effect on global warming, we would need to build a minimum of 1,000 reactors worldwide. This is a wildly unrealistic scenario, given that the current growth in nuclear electricity is at about 4%, and investors refuse to buy into nuclear power's dubious economics.

Nuclear power presents unacceptable risks to life on this planet: Its small contribution to power is far outweighed by its inherent dangers.

After half a century of producing deadly long-lived radioactive waste, not one country in the world has a method of isolating these wastes from the environment for the hundreds of thousands of years they will remain a threat. Monitoring and maintaining waste dumps over a period spanning 20 times the length of known civilisation is an unacceptable burden to place on all future generations—with no guarantees of long-term safety.

Even if it were climate-friendly, nuclear power could do little or nothing in the fight against global warming. Nuclear power is used only to generate electricity. It represents a mere 16% of the world's electricity. Electricity itself only accounts for approximately one-third of greenhouse gases.

Nuclear power presents unacceptable risks to life on this planet: Its small contribution to power is far outweighed by its inherent dangers. Nuclear power cannot deliver in the fight against global warming.

Tackling climate change effectively means reducing global greenhouse gas emissions by 50% by 2050. If we build more nuclear power plants, this would serve only to create more radioactive waste, more targets susceptible to terrorism and require massive expenditure of public subsidy. There are many more effective ways to reduce carbon emissions. For example, research carried out for the European Union concluded that when looking at the whole cycle of nuclear generation, from mining the uranium to decommissioning the plants, nuclear power stations would produce around 50% more greenhouse gas emissions than wind power.

Renewable Energy Potential Outstrips Nuclear

Many countries, such as the UK [United Kingdom], China, and Egypt, have enough wind power to meet their energy needs many times over. As tidal, wave, solar and biomass technologies develop, a diverse renewable energy industry will emerge. Even if it were climate-friendly, nuclear power could do little or nothing in the fight against global warming. Nuclear power is used only to generate electricity. It currently accounts for only 16% of the world's electricity while electricity itself only accounts for around one-third of greenhouse gases.

Rising Construction Times

Analysis undertaken by the World Energy Council has shown that worldwide construction times for nuclear reactors have increased. The average construction time for nuclear plants has increased from 66 months for completions in the mid-1970s, to 116 months (nearly 10 years) for completions between 1995 and 2000. The longer construction times are symptomatic of a range of problems, including managing the construction of increasingly complex reactor designs. In contrast, renewable energy is ready now and action to combat climate change needs to happen now. For example, the first offshore wind farm in the UK at North Hoyle in North Wales took only eight months to build.

MIT and other studies estimate that for nuclear power to have any effect on global warming, we would need to build a minimum of 1,000 reactors worldwide. This is a wildly unrealistic scenario, given that the current growth in nuclear electricity is at about 4%, and investors have yet to buy into nuclear power's uncertain financials.

Rising Construction Costs

The economic performance of nuclear power is heavily dependent on the construction costs, and delays in construction have had a significant impact on the economics of nuclear power. Interest on the capital borrowed to build the plant will increase with construction time. These economic problems can be seen in different regions around the world.

The economics of nuclear power have always been bad, and the industry only really got off the ground as a mask for nuclear weapons programmes.

In country after country nuclear construction programmes have gone considerably over budget. In the United States, an assessment of 75 of the country's reactors showed predicted costs to have been USD [U.S. dollars] 45 billion (€34bn [billion]) but the actual costs were USD 145 billion (€110bn). In India, the country with the most recent and current construction experience, completion costs of the last 10 reactors have averaged at least 300% over budget.

Falling Construction Demand

There are currently only 22 reactors under active construction in the world. The majority (17) are being built in Asia. Sixteen of the 22 are being built to Chinese, Indian or Russian designs, though none of these are likely to be exported to OECD countries. Construction on 5 reactors began over 20 years ago, which raises real doubts as to the likelihood of new reactors being built to their current timetable. There are a further 14 reactors on which construction is now suspended, 10 of which are in central and eastern Europe.

Rising Operational Costs

Nuclear power is not cheap. Costs associated with safety and security, insurance and liability in case of accident or attack, waste management, construction and decommissioning are rising substantially for nuclear power. The economics of nuclear power have always been bad, and the industry only really got off the ground as a mask for nuclear weapons programmes. The fact that consumers or governments have traditionally borne the risk of investment in nuclear power plants meant that utilities were insulated from these risks and were able to borrow money at rates reflecting a reduced risk.

However, following the introduction of competitive electricity markets in many countries, the risk that the plant would cost more than the forecast price was transferred to the power plant developers, who are constrained by the views of financial organisations such as banks, shareholders and credit rating agencies. Such organisations view investment in any type of power plant as risky. However, builders of non-nuclear power plants were willing to take these risks, as are vendors of energy efficiency services.

To install renewable energy generators is faster, cheaper and more reliable than the installation of nuclear power plants.

Consequently, when consumers no longer bear the economic risk of new plant construction, nuclear power, which combines uncompetitive high prices with poor reliability and serious risks of cost overruns, has no chance in countries that have moved to competitive power procurement. Any attempt to revive the nuclear industry would significantly undermine the growing confidence in renewable energy and divert funds away from real solutions to climate change.

The Nuclear Threat

Nuclear power provides the basic ingredients for nuclear weapons and dirty bombs, and provides an obvious target for terrorists. A global nuclear power construction programme large enough to achieve drastic greenhouse gas reductions would entail construction in all areas of the world, whether stable or not. Renewable energy installations on the other hand are flexible, cheap to construct and pose no terrorist or proliferation threat.

Nuclear technology, such as uranium enrichment is also used in nuclear weapons production, and therefore a proliferation risk. There are now more than 40 countries with civil nuclear power programmes, giving them the tools for nuclear weapons. Nuclear technology will always carry the risk that it will be used to construct weapons of mass destruction.

Untested Technology

The nuclear industry is promoting a new generation of reactors (Generation III and III+) and hoping that a wave of orders will be placed for them in the next few years. However, these are relatively untested and far from proven.

- *Generation III reactors*—The only Generation III reactors currently in operation are the Advanced Boiling Water Reactors (ABWRs) developed in Japan. By the end of 2006, four ABWRs were in service and two under construction in Taiwan. Total construction costs for the first two units were well above the forecast range. Further problems have now arisen as cracking has been found in the blades of the turbines of two plants.

- *Generation III+ reactors*—No Generation III+ plant has yet been completed and only one is under construction. The most widely promoted of these latest designs are the new generation of pressurized water reactors (PWRs), in particular AREVA's European Pressurized Reactor (EPR) and the Westinghouse AP1000.

- Other designs being developed include the Advanced CANDU Reactor (ACR-1000) and high temperature gas reactors (HTGRs). The most developed of the latter is a South African version of the Pebble Bed Modular Reactor (PBMR).

- *Generation IV reactors*—Even more speculative are the 'paper' designs for Generation IV plutonium-fuelled reactors. While several designs are being produced, technical difficulties make it unlikely they will be deployed for at least two decades, if at all, while the economics of fuel reprocessing also remain unproven.

Renewables—There Is No Alternative

Renewable energies could cover the global energy demand six times over with today's engineering—sustainably, peacefully, cleanly and infinitely. Every dollar invested in electricity efficiency displaces up to seven times as much carbon dioxide as a dollar invested in nuclear power.

There is no energy shortage. More energy falls on the earth each day than its 5.9 billion inhabitants would use in 27 years. Solar-generated power could provide the current world energy use 10,000 times over. Offshore wind in the North Sea alone could produce nearly twice the electricity needs of neighbouring countries.

To install renewable energy generators is faster, cheaper and more reliable than the installation of nuclear power plants. Construction time . . . for wind turbines is approximately two weeks, plus an average planning time of one to two years. Wind farms can "follow" growing demands from developing countries such as India and China easier than very slow and uncertain nuclear projects.

The German wind industry alone installed and generated more power within one decade than the nuclear industry did within a decade when they forced nuclear power onto the market. Most renewable energy technologies will be competitive against conventional fuels within the next 10 to 15 years—despite the massive subsidies still going to these conventional industries. Wind will be competitive within the next five to seven years—based on current fossil fuel prices. Oil, coal and gas prices have been rising for years and will continue to do so, as growing economies will increase their energy demand.

Case study: Olkiluoto 3 in Finland:

The Olkiluoto 3, an EPR construction project in Finland, is rapidly becoming an example of all that can go wrong in economic terms with nuclear new build. It demonstrates the key problems of construction delays due to safety concerns, cost overruns, as well as hidden state subsidies that are now facing various legal challenges. In December 2006, after only 16 months of construction, AREVA announced the reactor was already 18 months behind schedule, and it now seems likely that the project will fall at least €700m [million] over budget.

The Alternatives—Energy Efficiency and Renewables

There is enormous potential for reducing our consumption of energy, while providing the same level of energy 'services'. The Greenpeace Energy Revolution scenario details a series of energy efficiency measures, which together can substantially reduce demand in industries, homes, businesses and services. The solution to our future energy needs lies in greater use of renewable energy sources. Nuclear power is not the solution as it poses multiple threats to people and the environment.

The nuclear industry has seized on the problem of climate change to try to revive its dying industry. It argues that nuclear power can help achieve the dramatic cut in carbon emissions necessary to seriously address climate change, but the reality is that wasting yet more time and money pursuing the nuclear nightmare would be too late, too expensive, too risky, and could lead to nuclear weapons proliferation, because the majority of nuclear technologies and materials needed for a civil nuclear power programme are also essential to develop a nuclear weapons programme. The massive subsidies needed by the nuclear industry threaten to undermine the renewable energy revolution that is the real solution to climate change.

CHAPTER 4

What Is the Future of Nuclear Energy?

Chapter Preface

Nuclear reactor designs are classified into groups called generations. The term Generation I refers to the first prototype reactors built during the 1950s and 1960s. Generation II plants are those built in the 1970s and 1980s—typically water-cooled light water reactors, most of which are still in operation today. Generation III is a designation given to reactors built in recent years; most are water-cooled reactors with more advanced and safety features than early models. Generation IV refers to future reactor designs that, for the most part, have yet to be developed or built. Energy experts say these next generation reactors, by making improvements in safety and other features, could revamp the image of nuclear power and help to ensure that it will contribute to the world's future energy needs.

In 2001, nine countries—the United States, the United Kingdom, France, Argentina, Brazil, Canada, Japan, the Republic of Korea, and South Africa—formed the Generation IV International Forum (GIF) to research, develop, and implement these new nuclear technologies. After expert consultation, the group has agreed to promote six different types of Generation IV nuclear technologies, based on factors such as economics, safety, reliability, risk of nuclear proliferation, and the degree of physical protection from terrorism risks. The six reactor types include three different types of thermal reactors and three types of so-called fast reactors. Thermal reactors are the type of reactors generally employed in the past; they slow the neutrons that are used to create the fission reaction with control rods and are usually cooled by water. Fast reactors create fission reactions using high-energy neutrons, use no neutron control system, and use other types of coolants. The fast reactor process can extract much more energy from uranium fuel than thermal reactors; today's light water reactors, for example, typically use less than 1 percent of the fuel's potential energy. All the new designs incorporate safety features to prevent core overheating and the release of radioactive material— problems that have plagued the nuclear industry in the past.

The very high temperature reactor (VHTR), for example, is a helium-cooled thermal reactor with a core made from graphite, a substance that stays strong and stable even when the reactor reaches extremely high temperatures—approaching 900 degrees Celsius (1652 degrees Fahrenheit). In addition, the reactor uses uranium fuel particles that are coated with graphite so they will not crack or release fission products, no matter how high the heat. These safety features cause the nuclear reactions inside the core to naturally slow down as temperatures rise, thus preventing the reactor from ever melting down the way the reactor did in the Chernobyl disaster. These features also allow the helium coolant to be heated to temperatures three times as high as coolant in existing reactors, making it as much as 40 percent more efficient than older U.S. reactors. The VHTR's high heat also means it can be used for purposes other than electricity production, such as water desalination or the production of hydrogen for use as a transportation fuel. Research on this reactor type is already in progress in South Africa, Japan, France, the Republic of Korea, and the United States. In 2005, the U.S. Department of Energy authorized a prototype plant to be built by the Idaho National Laboratory. It should be completed between 2018 and 2021.

Another high-temperature Generation IV thermal reactor is the supercritical water-cooled reactor (SCWR). This system is water-cooled like previous light water reactors (LWRs) but it operates at higher temperatures (374 degrees Celsius or 705 degrees Fahrenheit) and is more efficient than the older water-cooled plants. In addition, SCWR plants are simpler to build than LWRs because the high temperatures mean that they do not require recirculation and jet pumps, pressurizers, steam generators, and other components needed to manage the water coolant in LWRs. This reactor design is also advantageous because it uses existing light water technology already in use and understood around the world.

A third type of thermal reactor is the molten salt reactor (MSR), a liquid-fueled design that can be used for producing electricity or hydrogen. Uranium and plutonium fuel is dissolved in a high-temperature fluoride salt that has a very high boiling temperature of about 1400 degrees Celsius (2552 degrees Fahrenheit). The liquid fuel then flows through a graphite reactor core, where fission occurs to produce heat. The liquid fuel has many advantages: For example, the fluoride salt is chemically stable, making the system very safe to operate; no fuel fabrication is required as in the VHTR reactor; and the system allows for adding or removing fuel and reprocessing of wastes while the plant is in operation.

The gas-cooled fast reactor (GFR) is a fast reactor design that features a fast neutron reactor, a helium-cooled system that reaches about 85 degrees Celsius (185 degrees Fahrenheit), and a closed fuel cycle that reprocesses spent fuel. Reprocessing substantially reduces the amount of waste produced and also reduces its radioactive decay time—from several thousand years to several hundred years. This design is attractive, therefore, because it greatly minimizes the amount of radioactive waste. Also, the GFR is very efficient, and like the SCWR system, it is simple to build and does not need steam components.

The sodium-cooled fast reactor (SFR), however, is the leading type of fast reactor design. The SFR uses a liquid sodium coolant, which is considered very safe because it works under normal atmospheric pressure and has a closed fuel system that reduces radioactive wastes. The SFR can also be built in various sizes, making it more economically competitive than many other reactor designs. A few early versions of SFRs already exist in the United States and Russia, but researchers are still perfecting the Generation IV SFR designs, therefore an improved SFR plant will probably not be built for at least a decade.

A third type of fast reactor is the lead-cooled fast reactor (LFR). This design is very safe because it uses a molten lead or lead/bismuth coolant, a material that is even less chemically reactive than sodium. Like the SFR and the GFR, it has a closed fuel cycle that allows for reprocessing of wastes, but unlike other fast reactors the LFR operates at a very high temperature, which may mean it can be used for both electricity and hydrogen production. Finally, the LFR uses liquid fuel dissolved in fluorides of lithium, beryllium, sodium or other elements, which allows for new fuel to be added during reactor operation and avoids the need for any type of fuel fabrication.

The hope is that Generation IV designs will be much more efficient and safer than older nuclear plants and will produce much less radioactive waste, providing an alternative to fossil fuels and a viable way to reduce the world's carbon emissions. The viewpoints in this chapter explore the possibilities for nuclear energy in the future.

A Nuclear Energy Comeback Faces Challenges in America

Paul Davidson

Paul Davidson is a reporter for USA Today, *a daily American newspaper.*

The nation's nuclear power industry—stuck in a decades-long deep freeze—is thawing.

Utilities are poised to build a new generation of nuclear plants 30 years after the Three Mile Island accident, whose anniversary was Saturday [March 28, 2009], halted new reactor applications. The momentum is being driven by growing public acceptance of relatively clean nuclear energy to combat global warming.

Several companies have taken significant steps that will likely lead to completion of four reactors by 2015 to 2018 and up to eight by 2020. All would be built next to existing nuclear plants.

Southern Co. (SO) says it will begin digging an 86-foot-deep crater this June in Vogtle, Ga., to make way for two reactors after recently winning state approval, though it won't pour concrete until it gets a federal license, likely in 2011. At least five power companies have signed contracts with equipment vendors. And Florida and South Carolina residents this year began paying new utility fees to finance planned reactors.

The steps signal that a nuclear renaissance anticipated for several years is finally taking shape. Seventeen companies have sought U.S. federal approval for 26 reactors since late 2007. All have enhanced safety features.

Paul Davidson, "Nuclear Power Inches Back into Energy Spotlight," *USA Today*, March 30, 2009. Reprinted with permission from USA TODAY, a division of Gannett Co., Inc.

"The resurgence of nuclear energy is under way," says Steve Kerekes of the Nuclear Energy Institute [NEI], an industry trade group.

Whether it will yield a flood of new reactors or a trickle will largely depend on the success—or failure—of the initial wave.

Utilities are poised to build a new generation of nuclear plants 30 years after the Three Mile Island accident . . . halted new reactor applications.

Nuclear a "Better Option" Now?

The industry believes it can avoid the billions in cost overruns and years of delays that marred nuclear construction in the 1970s and 1980s. Licensing has been streamlined. Utilities are seeking firmer costs and schedules. And designs are more detailed.

Still, some hurdles are emerging. Some companies are submitting incomplete applications or seeking design changes at the U.S. Nuclear Regulatory Commission (NRC), possibly delaying approval. At least two utilities recently said they're switching to different reactor models because they couldn't receive assurances on costs and the timetable. And since several models are new, problems could emerge as they're built in the USA for the first time. The type of reactor planned for Maryland is being built in Finland, where it's three years behind schedule and $2 billion over budget.

"We're talking about a new generation of technology," says John Reed, CEO of Concentric Energy Advisors. "You have to demonstrate to (lenders) that you can make money with these."

Nuclear plants are hugely expensive, and the credit crisis has all but sealed lenders' wallets. The success of the resurgence also hinges on companies' ability to obtain financing.

Nuclear officials are taking comfort in some encouraging signals from the Obama administration. During his campaign, then–candidate Barack Obama seemed cool to nuclear energy, saying waste storage concerns must be solved before the nation builds new plants. Although the new administration has said Yucca Mountain northwest of Las Vegas [Nevada] is no longer a storage option for the waste, Energy Secretary Steven Chu told Congress this month that nuclear "has to be" part of "our energy future." Waste, he said, can be stored at reactor sites "for decades."

The [nuclear] industry believes it can avoid the billions in cost overruns and years of delays that marred nuclear construction in the 1970s and 1980s.

Unlike power plants fueled by coal and even cleaner natural gas, nuclear reactors emit none of the heat-trapping gases blamed for global warming. Obama strongly favors capping global warming emissions from fossil fuel plants, which would boost nuclear's prospects. Renewable energy is popular but intermittent.

Today, 104 reactors supply 20% of the nation's electricity. Just to hold that share, all 26 proposed reactors would have to be completed by 2030. And to meet global warming goals, 42 reactors should be built the next two decades, according to the Electric Power Research Institute. Reed says that's possible if the first wave goes well. A new Gallup poll shows a record 59% of Americans favor nuclear energy.

Here's the rub: Nuclear reactor costs have doubled in the past three years to as much as about $8 billion, Moody's Investors Service says. They're twice as expensive as coal-fired plants and triple the cost of natural gas plants. Reactors also are far more complex, taking up to 10 years to license and build vs. a couple of years for gas-fired plants.

Yet, nuclear plants are far less costly to operate, and the fuel, uranium, is cheaper than coal and natural gas. South Carolina Electric & Gas [SCE&G] chose nuclear instead of natural gas to meet some of its power needs because it could produce electricity at retail rates of about 8 cents a kilowatt-hour vs. about 10 cents with gas. That's after figuring in subsidies such as production tax credits and before adding potential fees on gas plants for emitting CO_2.

"Nuclear came out to be a better option," says Stephen Byrne, nuclear chief for SCE&G, which plans two reactors near Columbia, S.C. "The cost of natural gas fluctuates pretty wildly."

Trying to Avoid Past Mistakes

The industry is recovering from a harrowing past. After the Three Mile Island accident in central Pennsylvania—which led to no deaths or known injuries, but caused a small radiation leak from the plant—the NRC passed sweeping new safety rules. Inspectors forced utilities to rip out pipes and install backup pumps or generators mid-construction. Since utilities didn't submit designs before building, each reactor was custom-built, further burdening the NRC.

Companies built plants so quickly to meet rising power demand that blueprints were only about 20% complete when construction began. Contractors redid work on the fly, causing delays. Double-digit interest rates drove up already swollen costs.

Compounding the problem: The NRC first issued a license to build a reactor, then a separate license to operate it. Utilities that completed plants had to wait for an operating license before they could sell electricity and recoup their investments.

Nationwide, state regulators denied utilities' petitions to recover $18 billion in cost overruns. Some went bankrupt.

Under new rules, power companies can apply for one license to both build and operate a nuclear reactor, streamlining the review. Designs must be approved separately before construction begins. And power companies are using just five blueprints. Regulators hope they'll churn out cookie-cutter versions of each design. Yet, even as they seek licenses, only two of the five designs have been certified.

Nuclear officials are taking comfort in some encouraging signals from the Obama administration.

"They're putting the cart before the horse," NRC Commissioner Gregory Jaczko says. "They should get the design done" before applying for a license. Also, he says, some reactor makers are proposing extensive modifications to their designs. Westinghouse, for instance, wants to make about 100 changes to its AP1000 reactor, says Vice President Ed Cummins. He says they're largely minor.

Other key challenges:

On time, within budget. To avoid cost overruns, power companies want to lock in prices and put the onus on equipment vendors to pay added fees if a project is delayed. Vendors are reluctant to set prices because the reactors lack a track record, and it's impossible to predict the cost of labor and materials when construction starts in a few years.

NRG [Energy], an independent power producer that's building two reactors in Texas, has signed a contract with Toshiba that nails down most costs, says Steven Winn, CEO of the NRG unit building the plant. That's possible, he says, because Toshiba owns 12% of the venture and has already built four of the same model units, called an ABWR [Advanced Boiling Water Reactor], in Japan.

Others are having mixed success at locking in terms. Exelon, for instance, recently said it was no longer going to use a General Electric Hitachi reactor because GE couldn't sufficiently guarantee fixed prices and a firm schedule. "We have to be careful and pragmatic" about risks, says GE Vice President Danny Roderick.

Elusive financing. With lenders hesitant to take chances on nuclear energy, 10 companies seek a total of $93 billion in federal loan guarantees for new nuclear plants. But only $18.5 billion is available—enough to finance three or four projects.

NEI President Marvin Fertel told Congress this month that independent power producers would likely abandon projects if the entire $93 billion is not funded, slowing the nuclear revival.

Bill Wicker, spokesman for the Senate Energy Committee [Senate Committee on Energy and Natural Resources], says guarantees are meant to bankroll only the maiden versions of new models. No more than another $18 billion is likely to be funded, he says. "It's not like a bottomless cup of coffee."

Loan guarantees are less critical for regulated utilities, such as Southern Co. and SCE&G, that have state clearances to recover some of their costs from ratepayers before construction is completed. In Florida, Progress Energy (PGN) customers began paying an extra $14.53 a month in January to finance two reactors. Missouri is among states considering such cost-recovery legislation, but lawmakers are divided. Ameren says it won't build a new reactor without it. "You'd get laughed off Wall Street," says Senior Vice President Richard Mark.

Avoiding construction snafus. Manufacturers are trying to avoid the missteps of the first construction era. Three-dimensional computer images tell engineers precisely where pipes should go. GE and Westinghouse say 70% to 80% of their designs will be done before they break ground. And makers are increasingly building modular parts in the factory, cutting costs and minimizing mistakes on site. Westinghouse says 30% of its AP1000 reactor is modular.

Still, "When you're building (a new model) for the first time, yes, there's risk," says Jone-Lin Wang of Cambridge Energy Research Associates.

The delays and cost overruns plaguing AREVA's EPR [European Pressurized Reactor] unit in Finland were partly related to concrete that failed inspection. "We're quite confident we're learning from" the Finnish experience, says Michael Wallace, chairman of UniStar, the Constellation Energy (CEG) unit building an EPR in Lusby, Md.

Tight supplies. Only one company, Japan Steel Works, builds the 600-ton steel forgings used to make reactor vessels. It can make only five or six a year. Southern Co., SCE&G, NRG and Constellation have spent tens of millions of dollars reserving such items. Those building reactors after the front-runners could face bottlenecks, Standard & Poor's says. But Japan Steel Works has said it's expanding its capacity by about a third, while others are entering the market. In the United States, factories to make nuclear parts are being built in Virginia, Louisiana, Indiana and Tennessee.

Fewer workers. New reactors are likely to strain a pool of nuclear workers depleted by the construction hiatus. About 100,000 new workers would be needed to build and staff the 26 proposed reactors. Meantime, 35% of the current workforce is eligible to retire in five years.

The NEI notes utilities have teamed with community colleges to train workers. Still, a likely shortage of specialized workers, such as nuclear welders, could drive up wages and construction costs, says consultant Steve Rus of Black & Veatch.

Overall, Reed says the risk of delays and cost overruns is "far less" now. Yet, some companies are waiting before deciding to build. In Texas, Luminant says it will monitor the status of natural gas prices and carbon caps. Ameren wants to see if the first plants are successful. That's why the utility didn't want "to be in that first wave of plants," says Ameren nuclear executive Scott Bond.

Nuclear Energy Use Must Be Increased to Reduce Carbon Emissions

MIT Energy Initiative

The MIT Energy Initiative (MITEI) seeks to transform the global energy system to meet the needs of the future and to facilitate that endeavor by improving energy systems currently in place.

In 2003 a group of MIT [Massachusetts Institute of Technology] faculty issued a study on *The Future of Nuclear Power*. The study was motivated by growing concern about global warming and the urgency of developing and deploying electricity-generating technologies that do not emit CO_2 or other greenhouse gases (GHG). The study addressed the steps needed in the near term in order to enable nuclear power to be a viable marketplace option at a time and at a scale that could materially mitigate climate change risks. In this context, the study explicitly assessed the challenges of a scenario in which nuclear power capacity expands from approximately 100 GWe [gigawatt electricity] in the United States in 2000 to 300 GWe at mid-century (from 340 to 1000 GWe globally), thereby enabling an increase in nuclear power's approximately 20% share of U.S. electricity generation to about 30% (from 16% to 20% globally).

The important challenges examined were (1) cost, (2) safety, (3) waste management, and (4) proliferation risk. In addition, the report examined technology opportunities and needs, and offered recommendations for research, development, and demonstration.

John M. Deutch, Charles W. Forsberg, Andrew C. Kadak, Mujid S. Kazimi, Ernest J. Moniz, John E. Parsons, Du Yangbo, and Lara Pierpoint of the MIT Energy Initiative, *Update of the MIT 2003 Future of Nuclear Power Study*, Massachusetts Institute of Technology, 2009. Reproduced by permission.

The 2003 MIT study on *The Future of Nuclear Power*, supported by the Alfred P. Sloan Foundation, has had a significant impact on the public debate both in the United States and abroad, and the study has influenced both legislation by the U.S. Congress and the U.S. Department of Energy's (DOE) nuclear energy R&D [research and development] program.

Nuclear power, ... carbon ... sequestration, and renewable energy technologies ... are important options for achieving electricity production with small carbon footprints.

This report presents an update on the 2003 study. Almost six years have passed since the report was issued, a new administration in Washington is formulating its energy policy, and, most importantly, concern about the energy future remains high. We review what has changed from 2003 to today with respect to the challenges facing nuclear power mentioned above. A second purpose of this update is to provide context for a new MIT study, currently under way, on *The Future of the Nuclear Fuel Cycle*, which will examine the pros and cons of alternative fuel cycle strategies, the readiness of the technologies needed for them, and the implications for near-term policies.

Summary Finding of Changes Since the 2003 Report

Concern with avoiding the adverse consequences of climate change has increased significantly in the past five years. The United States has not adopted a comprehensive climate change policy, although President [Barack] Obama is pledged to do so. Nor has an agreement been reached with the emerging rapidly growing economies such as China, India, Indonesia, and Mexico, about when and how they will adopt greenhouse gas emission constraints. With global greenhouse gas emissions projected to continue to increase, there is added urgency both to achieve greater energy efficiency and to pursue all measures to develop and deploy carbon-free energy sources.

More rapid progress is needed in enabling the option of nuclear power expansion to play a role in meeting the global warming challenge.

Nuclear power, fossil fuel use accompanied by carbon dioxide capture and sequestration, and renewable energy technologies (wind, biomass, geothermal, hydro and solar) are important options for achieving electricity production with small carbon footprints. Since the 2003 report, interest in using electricity for plug-in hybrids and electric cars to replace motor gasoline has increased, thus placing an even greater importance on exploiting the use of carbon-free, electricity-generating technologies. At the same time, as discussed in the MIT report *The Future of Coal*, little progress has been made in the United States in demonstrating the viability of fossil fuel use with carbon capture and sequestration—a major "carbon-free" alternative to nuclear energy for baseload electricity.

With regard to nuclear power, while there has been some progress since 2003, increased deployment of nuclear power has been slow both in the United States and globally, in relation to the illustrative scenario examined in the 2003 report. While the intent to build new plants has been made public in several countries, there are only few firm commitments outside of Asia, in particular China, India, and Korea, to construction projects at this time. Even if all the announced plans for new nuclear power plant construction are realized, the total will be well behind that needed for reaching a thousand gigawatts of new capacity worldwide by 2050. In the United States, only one shutdown reactor has been refurbished and restarted, and one previously ordered, but never completed re-actor, is now being completed. No new nuclear units have started construction.

In sum, compared to 2003, the motivation to make more use of nuclear power is greater, and more rapid progress is needed in enabling the option of nuclear power expansion to play a role in meeting the global warming challenge. The so-ber warning is that if more is not done, nuclear power will di-minish as a practical and timely option for deployment at a scale that would constitute a material contribution to climate change risk mitigation.

Nuclear Energy Expansion is Unrealistic

Charles D. Ferguson

Charles D. Ferguson is a fellow for science and technology at the Council on Foreign Relations, an independent public policy organization. He is also an adjunct assistant professor in the School of Foreign Service at Georgetown University and an adjunct lecturer at Johns Hopkins University.

According to a prevailing belief, humanity confronts two stark risks: catastrophes caused by climate change and annihilation by nuclear war. The conventional wisdom also believes that the former danger appears far more certain than the latter. This assessment has recently led an increasing number of policy makers, pundits, businesspeople, and environmentalists to advocate a major expansion of nuclear energy, which emits very few greenhouse gases into the atmosphere. While acknowledging the connection between nuclear fuel making and nuclear bomb building, nuclear power proponents suggest that nuclear proliferation and terrorism risks are readily manageable. Consequently, some of these advocates favor the use of subsidies to stimulate substantial growth of nuclear power.

This conventional wisdom possesses some truth, but it oversells the contribution nuclear energy can make to reduce global warming and strengthen energy security while downplaying the dangers associated with this energy source. To realistically address global warming, the nuclear industry would have to expand at such a rapid rate as to pose serious concerns for how the industry would ensure an adequate supply of reasonably inexpensive reactor-grade construction materi-

Charles D. Ferguson, "Nuclear Energy: Balancing Benefits and Risks," Council Special Report No. 28, April 2007. Copyright © 2007 by the Council on Foreign Relations Press. Reproduced by permission.

als, well-trained technicians, and rigorous safety and security measures. Furthermore, some argue that a significant growth of nuclear reactors and fuel making in politically unstable regions would substantially increase the risks of nuclear terrorism and proliferation. Conversely, others decry the hypocrisy of this double standard in which only certain countries are allowed access to the full suite of nuclear technologies. Thus, the United States faces a fundamental policy dilemma: Is it possible to encourage growth of nuclear energy and fuel making in some regions and countries while denying or significantly limiting it in other places?

Nuclear Energy at a Crossroads

To reduce the deleterious effects of climate change, the world will need to dramatically increase the use of low- and no-carbon emission energy sources as well as promote far greater use of energy efficiencies. Nuclear will undoubtedly be part of this mix, but the policy question is: How much can and should it contribute to energy needs? This benefit needs to be weighed against the entire costs and risks of nuclear power production.

[Nuclear proponents] oversell ... the contribution nuclear energy can make to reduce global warming ... while downplaying the dangers associated with this energy source.

In addition to substantial capital costs for construction of power plants, nuclear energy includes significant external costs: applying safeguards to sensitive activities such as fuel making, securing nuclear facilities against terrorist attacks, decommissioning reactors, storing highly radioactive waste, and paying for insurance to cover the costs of an accident. Another important policy question is: How much of these external costs should be paid for by the industry versus governments? A related question is: If all energy sectors identified and paid for most, if not all, of their external costs, including greenhouse gas emissions, how would the nuclear sector fare on this level playing field that refrained from further government subsidies? . . .

The United States has considerably more leverage influencing domestic nuclear energy production than international use; however, the United States can help shape nuclear policies abroad through leading by example and through making use of existing bilateral partnerships and multilateral institutions, including the International Atomic Energy Agency, the International Energy Agency, and the Nuclear Suppliers Group. An effective policy needs to address climate change, energy security, safety and security of nuclear power plants and radioactive waste storage, and proliferation of nuclear technologies that can produce nuclear bombs. . . .

Nuclear Energy's Role in Strengthening U.S. Energy Security

Nuclear power can provide greater energy security by reducing reliance on fossil fuels acquired from unstable regions. In recent years, the United States imported about two-thirds of its oil and one-fifth of its natural gas. Most of the oil the United States uses fuels transportation needs with only a small portion (about 3 percent) used for generating electricity. Electricity generation from all sources comprises about 40 percent of total U.S. energy consumption. Of this total, nuclear comprises only about 8 percent. Currently, nuclear power, which solely generates electricity, offers some relief in use of foreign sources of oil and natural gas and could, over the long term (many decades), power cars and trucks through production of hydrogen for fuel cells or electricity for plug-in hybrid vehicles. But at least over the next few decades, a substantial growth in nuclear energy use will not wean the United States off foreign sources of oil.

Unlike oil, natural gas provides a significant portion (16 percent) of U.S. electricity production as well as heating for homes and businesses. Rising natural gas prices, however, have sparked recent corporate interest in nuclear power. If natural gas prices remain at the currently high levels for many years, nuclear power could offer a more favorable business investment. But historically, natural gas prices have fluctuated, and the presently high prices could fall, undermining support for a growth of nuclear energy.

In addition to substantial capital costs for construction of power plants, nuclear energy includes significant external costs.

In the electricity-production sector, nuclear power plants' operating costs compete favorably with coal, natural gas, hydro, oil, geothermal, wind, and solar energy sources, but its capital costs have difficulty competing against them. Presently, according to the Energy Information Administration, the United States produces 52 percent of its electricity from coal-fired plants, 21 percent from nuclear power plants, 16 percent from natural gas, 7 percent from hydro, 3 percent from oil, and 1 percent from geothermal, wind, and solar combined. Thus, the vast majority of U.S. electricity comes from three sources: coal, nuclear, and natural gas. . . . Coal remains a relatively cheap fuel, and capital costs for coal-fired plants are considerably less than for nuclear plants. The United States is the Saudi Arabia of coal reserves; thus, the use of coal helps reduce dependence on foreign sources of oil and natural gas in the electricity-production sector. Without restrictions imposed on greenhouse gas emissions, coal wins out over nuclear in terms of financial costs.

Economics is a major factor influencing the growth of nuclear energy. As an industry official recently said, "Nuclear energy is a business, not a religion." Despite the passions both for and against continued or expanded use of this energy source, business decisions will mainly determine whether use of nuclear-generated electricity will rise or fall.

The long lead time for, and large uncertainties in, nuclear reactor construction and licensing have stymied growth in the industry in the United States. American utilities have not ordered a nuclear reactor since 1978, and that order was subsequently canceled. The last completed reactor in the United States was the Tennessee Valley Authority's Watts Bar 1, which was ordered in 1970 and began operation in 1996.

An effective policy needs to address climate change, energy security, safety and security of nuclear power plants and radioactive waste storage, and [nuclear] proliferation.

Despite the lack of reactor orders, the contribution of nuclear-generated electricity has increased in recent years in the United States. During the past decade, average operating costs have decreased, and time needed for refueling outages has shortened, allowing nuclear power plants to operate longer at full capacity or, in industry terms, "increasing the load factor." Moreover, several nuclear plants have received licenses to increase their power ratings, again permitting production of more electricity.

While the industry has yet to order any new domestic reactors, changes in U.S. law have helped renew interest among several companies in applying for reactor licenses. The Energy Policy Act of 1992 began a reform of the licensing process to allow combining construction and operating licenses in one application. In principle, a combined license should help streamline the application process. Yet, large uncertainties in construction costs continue to impede investors. To try to jump-start the nuclear industry, which was already receiving more subsidies than any other no- and low-carbon energy sources, the Energy Policy Act of 2005 provided billions of additional dollars' worth of incentives to nuclear and smaller amounts of incentives to other no- and low-carbon energy sources. Nonetheless, the process of new nuclear reactor licensing and construction is estimated to take ten to fifteen years. Even if their license applications are approved, the utilities have still not committed to building the reactors.

In the coming decades, the U.S. nuclear industry will have to run faster on the treadmill of impending nuclear power plant retirements to replace the aging fleet of reactors.

In the coming decades, the U.S. nuclear industry will have to run faster on the treadmill of impending nuclear power plant retirements to replace the aging fleet of reactors. Initially, commercial reactors received forty-year licenses. While a number of reactors never reached their forty-year nominal life spans before being decommissioned, much of the current fleet of reactors has, in recent years, received twenty-year license renewals. As of the end of 2006, more than forty reactors have obtained twenty-year license extensions and about a dozen more have applied for renewal. [Data] . . . show that even assuming all 103 currently operating reactors receive twenty-year license renewals and no new reactors are constructed, the U.S. fleet will cease operations by 2056.

Without new reactor construction, a precipitous falloff will begin about twenty years from now. While U.S. Nuclear Regulatory Commission (NRC) Chairman Dale E. Klein has recently discussed considering license renewals for up to eighty total years for a selected number of reactors, prudent planning would suggest counting on replacing practically all of the current reactors within the coming decades. The replacement rate would be on the order of one new reactor every four to five months over the next forty years. Based on the periods of the

1960s and 1970s, when most of the current fleet was built, this construction rate appears feasible. However, based on the past thirty years, in which reactor orders and construction ground to a halt, this replacement rate faces daunting challenges. For this reason alone, nuclear energy is not a major part of the solution to U.S. energy insecurity for at least the next fifty years. . . .

Recommendations

Nuclear energy produces one-fifth of U.S. electricity and one-sixth of global electricity; thus, the United States and its partners have a vested interest in ensuring safe and secure operation of the world's nuclear industry. But the future of domestic and international commercial nuclear energy use faces large uncertainties in financial competitiveness and in external costs such as proliferation risks of the nuclear fuel cycle, safe and secure operation of nuclear power plants, and long-term disposal of highly radioactive waste. Generating electricity from any energy source comes with external costs. Traditionally, the U.S. government and many other governments have relied on subsidies to pick winners and losers among energy sectors. But providing subsidies to mature industries such as nuclear power have hidden the external costs. Governments should strive to identify and factor in as many of the external costs as possible into the price of energy sources.

While nuclear energy will continue to play a role in meeting the world's energy needs, it will not solve the immediate problems of climate change.

One of the biggest external costs is environmental damage from greenhouse gas emissions. The United States must work urgently to achieve the objective of substantially reducing global warming as fast as possible and thus should shift from providing subsidies to holding all energy sectors equally accountable for their external costs. Currently, the costs incurred through carbon pollution are a debt unpaid; therefore, governments should begin by collecting these costs through a mechanism such as imposing a fee on greenhouse gas emissions. In other words, the polluter pays. This step would act to level the economic playing field among high-carbon emitters such as traditional coal-fired plants and no- and low-carbon emitters such as highly efficient natural gas plants, nuclear plants, and wind- and solar-generated electricity. No single energy source is a technical panacea for combating global warming. Also, there are too many uncertainties in having governments pick the correct mix of energy sources to achieve the goal of countering the worst effects of climate change. However, a price, in some form, imposed on carbon emissions would stimulate the market to work toward an appropriate mix. Nuclear power will remain part of this mix for the foreseeable future.

While nuclear energy will continue to play a role in meeting the world's energy needs, it will not solve the immediate problems of climate change. To effectively counter climate change, the United States and its partners must move quickly forward to advance the use of all low- and no-carbon forms of energy, to use energy more efficiently, and to develop methods of capturing and storing carbon emissions. Over the long term, an economically competitive nuclear industry could experience modest growth domestically and internationally. The United States and its partners should welcome such growth provided they can successfully manage nuclear energy's risks: safety, security, waste disposal, and proliferation.

Nuclear Power's Multiple Limitations Will Constrain Its Future Growth

Joseph Romm

Joseph Romm is an American author, blogger, physicist, and climate expert. He is also a senior fellow at the Center for American Progress Action Fund, a progressive think tank.

Nuclear power generates approximately 20 percent of all U.S. electricity. And because it is a low-carbon source of around-the-clock power, it has received renewed interest as concern grows over the effect of greenhouse gas emissions on our climate.

Yet nuclear power's own myriad limitations will constrain its growth, especially in the near term. These include:

- Prohibitively high, and escalating, capital costs

- Production bottlenecks in key components needed to build plants

- Very long construction times

- Concerns about uranium supplies and importation issues

- Unresolved problems with the availability and security of waste storage

- Large-scale water use amid shortages

- High electricity prices from new plants

Nuclear power is therefore unlikely to play a dominant—greater than 10 percent—role in the national or global effort

Joseph Romm, *The Self-Limiting Future of Nuclear Power*, Center for American Progress Action Fund, June 2008. www.americanprogressaction.org. This material was created by the Center for American Progress Action Fund.

to prevent the global temperatures from rising by more than 2°C above preindustrial levels.

The carbon-free power technologies that the nation and the world should focus on deploying right now at large scale are efficiency, wind power, and solar power. They are the lower-cost carbon-free strategies with minimal societal effects and the fewest production bottlenecks. They could easily meet all of U.S. demand for the next quarter-century, while substituting for some existing fossil fuel plants. In the medium term (post-2020), other technologies, such as coal with carbon capture and storage or advanced geothermal, could be significant players, but only with a far greater development effort over the next decade.

Nuclear power is . . . unlikely to play a dominant—greater than 10 percent—role in the national or global effort to prevent [global warming].

Progressives must also focus on the issue of nuclear subsidies, or nuclear pork. Conservative politicians such as Sen. John McCain (R-AZ) and other nuclear power advocates continue to insist that new climate legislation must include yet more large subsidies for nuclear power. Since nuclear power is a mature electricity-generation technology with a large market share and is the beneficiary of some $100 billion in direct and indirect subsidies since 1948, it neither requires nor deserves significant subsidies in any future climate law.

The High Cost of Nuclear Power

For three decades, no new nuclear power plants have been ordered in the United States. Now a number of utilities are proposing to build nuclear power plants, in large part because of the escalating cost of electricity from new fossil fuels plants and the federal government's promise of production tax credits and loan guarantees for investments in new nuclear power capacity.

Nuclear power has reemerged as a major issue in the policy and political arenas in large part because of the growing recognition that the nation and the world must make significant reductions in greenhouse gas emissions. The combustion of fossil fuels is the primary source of carbon dioxide, which is the main greenhouse gas.

The threat of catastrophic global warming means that no carbon-free source of power can be rejected out of hand. The very serious possibilities that sea levels will rise several inches each decade for many centuries, and a third of the planet will undergo desertification are far graver concerns than the very genuine environmental concerns about radiation releases and long-term waste issues.

The issue of whether we should invest in nuclear power has typically been fought on classic partisan grounds, with progressives being skeptical and conservatives being enthusiastic. Conservative Sen. John McCain (R-AZ) has repeatedly said that nuclear power is the centerpiece of his climate strategy, and that the United States should emulate the French, who get 80 percent of their power from nuclear. Newt Gingrich has recently proposed a similar commitment to nuclear power. Progressives counter that this plan would require building several hundred more new nuclear power plants and several Yucca Mountain–sized nuclear waste storage sites by 2050 at a total cost of more than $4 trillion.

Nuclear power is hampered by a variety of problems that limit its viability as a climate strategy absent massive government subsidies and mandates, especially in the near term. As a 2003 interdisciplinary study by the Massachusetts Institute of Technology [MIT] on *The Future of Nuclear Energy* concluded, "The prospects for nuclear energy as an option are limited . . . by four unresolved problems: high relative costs; perceived adverse safety, environmental, and health effects; potential security risks stemming from proliferation; and unresolved challenges in long-term management of nuclear wastes."

New nuclear power now costs more than double what the MIT report assumed in its base case, making it perhaps the most significant "unresolved problem." It is easily the most important issue and is the source of much confusion in the popular press. Consider this recent interview between *Newsweek*'s Fareed Zakaria and Patrick Moore, one of the co-founders of Greenpeace and now a strong nuclear advocate. Zakaria says, "A number of analyses say that nuclear power isn't cost competitive, and that without government subsidies, there's no real market for it." Moore replies, "That's simply not true. . . . I know that the cost of production of electricity among the 104 nuclear plants operating in the United States is 1.68 cents per kilowatt-hour. That's not including the capital costs, but the cost of production of electricity from nuclear is very low, and competitive with dirty coal. Gas costs three times as much as nuclear, at least. Wind costs five times as much, and solar costs 10 times as much."

Nuclear power is hampered by a variety of problems that limit its viability as a climate strategy absent massive government subsidies and mandates, especially in the near term.

Moore's answer states a common misconception—that you can ignore capital cost when calculating the cost of energy. His statement would be like saying, "My house is incredibly cheap to live in, if I don't include the mortgage." If you don't include the capital costs, then wind and solar [energy] are essentially free—nobody charges for the fuel, and operation is cheap. Compare this to nuclear plants, which are probably the most capital-intensive form of energy there is; also, they run on expensive uranium and must be closely monitored minute by minute for safety reasons. . . .

The Challenge of Building Plants Fast Enough

To avoid the grave risks posed by global temperatures rising more than 2°C above preindustrial levels, we must stabilize atmospheric concentrations of carbon dioxide below 450 parts per million [ppm].

As of the end of 2007, atmospheric CO_2 concentrations were already at 385 ppm. The concentration has been rising at a rate of 2 ppm a year since 2000, which is a 40 percent higher rate than the previous two decades. Global carbon dioxide emissions are more than 8 billion metric tons of carbon—29 billion metric tons of CO_2—and have been rising some 3 percent per year. To stay below 450 ppm, the latest analysis from the IPCC [Intergovernmental Panel on Climate Change] says that we should average under 5 billion tons of carbon a year for the entire century. So we need to peak in emissions globally in the 2015 to 2020 time frame and return to 4 billion metric tons of carbon or less by 2050.

Reducing emissions to the necessary levels will require some 14 (modified) "stabilization wedges," the term coined by Princeton's Robert Socolow and Stephen Pacala for an "activity that reduces emissions to the atmosphere that starts at zero today and increases linearly until it accounts for 1 GtC/year [one billion tons of carbon] of reduced carbon emissions in 50 years." Since the time for action is so short, the wedges probably need to be modified so that they are squeezed into about four decades.

Nuclear plants . . . are probably the most capital-intensive form of energy there is.

The most comprehensive report ever done on what one wedge of nuclear power would require is the 2007 Keystone Center report, *Nuclear Power Joint Fact-Finding*, which was supported by the utility and nuclear industries. The report notes that achieving a wedge of nuclear power by mid-century would require building approximately 1,000 1-GW [gigawatt, or one billion watts] nuclear plants, which requires adding globally:

- An average of 14 new plants each year for the next 50 years, as well as approximately 7.4 plants a year to replace those that will be retired.

- 11 to 22 additional large enrichment plants to supplement the 17 existing plants.

- 18 additional fuel fabrication plants to supplement the 24 existing plants.

- 10 nuclear waste repositories the size of the statutory capacity of Yucca Mountain, each of which would store approximately 700,000 tons of spent fuel.

In short, we need five decades of building nuclear plants at a rate only previously achieved for one decade—20 GW/year during the 1980s.

In fact, since we really need to deploy all this low-carbon power in 40 years, we should build 25 GW of nuclear plants a year.

Any individual wedge has a scale problem. One wedge of coal with carbon capture and storage will require storing the emissions from 800 large coal plants (80 percent of all coal plants in 2000). This represents a flow of CO_2 into the ground equal to the current flow of oil out of the ground. That would require recreating the equivalent of the planet's entire oil delivery infrastructure. One wedge of wind is 2,000 GW of nominal wind capacity. Last year the world installed 20 GW of wind.

Nuclear has a number of unique problems of scalability. Siting and building that many large waste repositories will not be easy, particularly given the difficulty that the United States has had siting a single one. On the other hand, reprocessing all the spent fuel would require 36 reprocessing plants, and add another 1.5 to 3 cents per kWh [kilowatt-hour] to the cost of nuclear electricity.

Nuclear Building Supplies Are Limited and Expensive

Then there are the industry bottlenecks. Twenty years ago the United States had 400 major suppliers for the nuclear industry. Today there are about 80. Only two companies in the whole world can make heavy forgings for pressure vessels, steam generators, and pressurizers that are licensed for use in any OECD [Organisation for Economic Co-operation and Development] country: Japan Steel Works and Creusot Forge.

Achieving a wedge of nuclear power by mid-century would require building approximately 1,000 ... nuclear plants.

Japan Steel is "the only plant in the world ... capable of producing the central part of a nuclear reactor's containment vessel in a single piece, reducing the risk of a radiation leak." In a single year, they can currently only make "four of the steel forgings that contain the radioactivity in a nuclear reactor." They may double capacity over the next two years, but that won't allow the huge ramp up in nuclear power that some are projecting for the industry.

According to Mycle Schneider, an independent nuclear industry consultant near Paris, the math just doesn't work given Japan Steel's limited capacity. Japan Steel caters to all nuclear reactor makers except in Russia, which makes its own heavy forgings. "I find it just amazing that so many people jumped on the bandwagon of this renaissance without ever looking at the industrial side of it," Schneider said.

At the same time, that capacity increase represents a gamble that the nuclear renaissance is here to stay, even in the face of rapidly escalating prices.

These supply bottlenecks, coupled with soaring commodity prices, have resulted in enormous price increases, even though new reactors have only been coming online at an average rate of about four to five per year in the past decade.

Uranium Is Becoming Harder to Find and Must Be Imported

Uranium supply is also an issue. Most major carbon-free power sources have no fuel concerns since they are renewable sources that ultimately draw their power from the sun, or they are energy-efficient technologies.

Uranium production, however, has had difficulty keeping up with demand. From 1989 through 2003, the industry average uranium spot price was in the $10 to $15 a pound range. It soared to over $135 a pound in 2007 and now is back down around $60 a pound as of mid-May.

There is a great deal of controversy as to whether "peak uranium" exists, a point at which production maxes out and then declines. The subject is beyond the scope of this [viewpoint], except to say that adding and sustaining one full wedge of nuclear power requires a near tripling of nuclear power generation and hence greatly increasing uranium demand. An article in the April 2008 *Environmental Science & Technology* concluded, "Given the broad coverage of uranium exploration globally over the past 50 years, any new deposit discovered is most likely to be deeper than most current deposits." What's more, "the long-term trend over the past five decades has been a steady decline in most average country ore grades.... In terms of major production capacity for any proposed nuclear power program, it is clear that these larger-tonnage, lower-grade deposits would need to be developed."

The other related issue for the United States is where we get our uranium from. In 2006, we imported 84 percent, or 56 million pounds, of our uranium. In February, the [George W.] Bush administration signed a deal to boost U.S. imports of Russian uranium: "The new agreement permits Russia to supply 20 percent of U.S. reactor fuel until 2020 and to supply the fuel for new reactors quota-free." Given that Russia has used its energy exports in the past for leverage against neighboring countries, this certainly raises energy security concerns for America.

Uranium production ... has had difficulty keeping up with demand.

If the United States were to significantly expand its use of nuclear power, doubling or tripling (or more) from current levels, our dependence on foreign sources of uranium and our trade deficit in uranium would likely grow significantly. If we seek to satisfy a significant portion of this increased demand from domestic uranium deposits, we run the risk, indeed the likelihood, given the sorry state of regulating U.S. uranium mining operations, of repeating the environmental debacle of the uranium boom that accompanied the build out of the U.S. nuclear arsenal and the first wave of nuclear power plant construction. Of course, for uranium mined in places like Russia, Kazakhstan, and Uzbekistan, we may surmise that there is no effective enforcement of environmental standards whatsoever, resulting in the likely extensive pollution of drinking water and agricultural aquifers with heavy metals and mining chemicals such as sulfuric acid, as well as lasting damage to the health of workers and surrounding populations.

Water Shortages Will Hamper Growth and Increase Costs

Finally, we have water consumption. As a 2008 Department of Energy report on wind power noted, "few realize that electricity generation accounts for nearly half of all water withdrawals in the nation." At the same time, "existing nuclear power stations used and consumed significantly more water per megawatt-hour than electricity generation powered by fossil fuels," as a 2002 report by the Electric Power Research Institute found.

Yet as a comprehensive 2006 Department of Energy report, *Energy Demands on Water Resources*, noted, "Some regions have seen groundwater levels drop as much as 300 to 900 feet over the past 50 years because of the pumping of water from aquifers faster than the natural rate of recharge. A 2003 General Accounting Office [now the Government Accountability Office] study showed that most state water managers expect either local or regional water shortages within the next 10 years under average climate conditions. Under drought conditions, even more severe water shortages are expected."

Merely replacing most of the existing reactors [in America] and around the world by 2050 will be a great and costly challenge.

Climate change is expected to drive drought, desertification, and water shortages (from the loss of the inland glaciers that feed major rivers) throughout the nation and the world. A 2006 analysis by the United Kingdom's Hadley Centre for Climate Prediction and Research found that on our current emissions path, we may see desertification of one-third of the planet and drought over half the planet by the end of the century.

A 2007 study published in *Science* warned of a permanent drought by 2050 throughout the Southwest—levels of aridity comparable to the 1930s Dust Bowl would stretch from Kansas to California. The Dust Bowl occurred due to a sustained decrease in soil moisture of about 15 percent, which is calculated by subtracting evaporation from precipitation. In some climate scenarios, soil moisture will decline 30 percent to 40 percent over much of the South and Southwest.

Clearly, future power plants need to be designed to use very little water. Nuclear power can be designed with dry (air) cooling driven by giant fans, but that increases capital costs and lowers the net electrical output of the plant. The 2006 Department of Energy report noted, "In total, dry-cooled systems impose a cost penalty ranging from 2 to 5 percent to 6 to 16 percent for the cost of energy compared to evaporative closed-loop cooling. These ranges reflect the fact that the cost penalty is highly dependent on the value placed on the energy that is not generated and must be replaced when the weather is hot and demand is high."

So, again, nuclear power can deal with the water issues, but only at a price penalty. As of 2002, "dry cooling had been installed on only a fraction of 1 percent of U.S. generating capacity, mostly on smaller plants."

Nuclear power will have great difficulty filling out even one of the 14 wedges needed to stabilize carbon dioxide concentrations below 450 ppm. Indeed, merely replacing most of the existing reactors here and around the world by 2050 will be a great and costly challenge. And given a long time lag for deploying reactors and rebuilding the industry, and the urgent need to reverse U.S. and global greenhouse gas emissions growth by 2020 and then sharply reduce emissions through 2050 and beyond, we must look seriously at carbon-free sources that might be deployed faster, cheaper, and with less accompanying problems.

The Future Viability of Nuclear Energy is Unclear

Lisbeth Gronlund, David Lochbaum, and Edwin Lyman

Lisbeth Gronlund is codirector and senior scientist of the Global Security Program, a project of the Union of Concerned Scientists (UCS), a science-based nonprofit organization. David Lochbaum is director of the nuclear safety project in the UCS Global Security Program. Edwin Lyman is a senior staff scientist in the UCS Global Security Program.

Global warming demands a profound transformation in the ways we generate and consume energy. Because nuclear power results in few global warming emissions, an increase in nuclear power could help reduce global warming—but it could also increase the threats to human safety and security. The risks include a massive release of radiation due to a power plant meltdown or terrorist attack, and the death of hundreds of thousands due to the detonation of a nuclear weapon made with materials obtained from a civilian nuclear power system. Minimizing these risks is simply pragmatic: Nothing will affect the public acceptability of nuclear power as much as a serious nuclear accident, a terrorist strike on a reactor or spent fuel pool, or the terrorist detonation of a nuclear weapon made from stolen nuclear reactor materials.

The report finds that:

1. The United States has strong nuclear power safety standards, but serious safety problems continue to arise at U.S. nuclear power plants because the U.S. Nuclear Regulatory Commission (NRC) is not adequately enforcing the existing standards. The NRC's poor safety culture is the biggest barrier to consistently effective over-

Lisbeth Gronlund, David Lochbaum, and Edwin Lyman, *Nuclear Power in a Warming World: Assessing the Risks, Addressing the Challenges*, Union of Concerned Scientists, December 2007. Reproduced by permission.

sight, and Congress should require the NRC to bring in
managers from outside the agency to rectify this problem.

2. While the United States has one of the world's most
well-developed regulatory systems for protection of
nuclear facilities against sabotage and attack, current
security standards are inadequate to defend against credible threats. Congress should give the responsibility for
identifying credible threats and ensuring that security is
adequate to the Department of Homeland Security
rather than the NRC.

3. The extent to which an expansion of nuclear power increases the risk that more nations or terrorists will acquire nuclear weapons depends largely on whether reprocessing is included in the fuel cycle, and whether
uranium enrichment comes under effective international
control. A global prohibition on reprocessing, and international ownership of all enrichment facilities, would
greatly reduce these risks. The United States should rein-
state a ban on reprocessing U.S. spent fuel and take the
lead in forging an indefinite global moratorium on reprocessing. The administration should also pursue a
regime to place all uranium enrichment facilities under
international control.

4. Over the next 50 years, interim storage of spent fuel in
dry casks is economically viable and secure, if hardened
against attack. In the longer term, a geologic repository
would provide the stability needed to isolate the spent
fuel from the environment. It is critical to identify and
overcome technical and political barriers to licensing a
permanent repository, and the Department of Energy
should identify and begin to characterize potential sites
other than Yucca Mountain [in Nevada].

5. Of all the new reactor designs being seriously considered for deployment in the United States, only one—the Evolutionary Power Reactor—appears to have the potential to be significantly safer and more secure than today's reactors. To eliminate any financial incentives for reactor vendors to reduce safety margins, and to make safer reactors competitive in the United States, the NRC should require new U.S. reactors to be significantly safer than current reactors.

6. The proposed Global Nuclear Energy Partnership (GNEP) plan offers no waste disposal benefits and would increase the risks of nuclear proliferation and terrorism. It should be dropped.

Since its founding in 1969, the Union of Concerned Scientists (UCS) has worked to make nuclear power safer and more secure. We have long sought to minimize the risk that nations and terrorists would acquire nuclear weapons materials from nuclear power facilities. This report shows that nuclear power continues to pose serious risks that are unique among the energy options being considered for reducing global warming emissions. The future risks of nuclear energy will depend in large part on whether governments, industry, and international bodies undertake a serious effort to address these risks . . . before plunging headlong into a rapid expansion of nuclear energy worldwide. In particular, the risks will increase—perhaps substantially—if reprocessing becomes part of the fuel cycle in the United States and expands worldwide.

An increase in nuclear power could help reduce global warming—but it could also increase the threats to human safety and security.

The risks posed by climate change may turn out to be so grave that the United States and the world cannot afford to rule out nuclear power as a major contributor to addressing global warming. However, it may also turn out that nuclear power cannot be deployed worldwide on the scale needed to make a significant dent in emissions without resulting in unacceptably high safety and security risks. Resolving these questions is beyond the scope of this [viewpoint], but ... [it can] inform a necessary discussion of the risks of various energy technologies that can address global warming.

National Nuclear Energy Oversight and International Safety Standards Are Essential for Its Expansion

Allison Macfarlane, James Asselstine, and John Ahearne

Allison Macfarlane is an associate professor of environmental science and policy at George Mason University; James Asselstine served as a commissioner on the U.S. Nuclear Regulatory Commission from 1982 to 1987 and formerly headed the electric utility fixed income research team at Lehman Brothers; and John Ahearne served as a commissioner on the U.S. Nuclear Regulatory Commission from 1978 to 1983 and has advised the U.S. government on a range of scientific and policy issues.

Global warming necessitates the development of new forms of low emissions, baseload power generating capacity. To assess the financial, regulatory, and proliferation concerns confronting nuclear energy and to develop strategies for addressing the barriers to the deployment of new reactors, in late September 2008, the Bulletin of the Atomic Scientists [an organization dedicated to global security] convened nearly 40 scientists, policy makers, industry representatives, and non-governmental experts from around the world. The meeting was cosponsored by the University of Chicago, Argonne National Laboratory, and the Chicago Council on Science and Technology.

A subset of the meeting's participants developed the following findings and recommendations based upon the presentations and discussions at the meeting. These findings and

Allison Macfarlane, James Asselstine, and John Ahearne, "The Future of Nuclear Energy: Policy Recommendations," *Bulletin of the Atomic Scientists*, December 11, 2008. Reproduced by permission of *Bulletin of the Atomic Scientists: The Magazine of Global Security News & Analysis*.

recommendations do not represent the views of all of the meeting participants or sponsors. . . .

- *Finding #1*: Recent efforts to license and build new nuclear reactors overseas, in Finland and France in particular, offer lessons for the United States regarding possible construction obstacles and cost and schedule overruns.

- *Recommendation #1*: The U.S. Nuclear Regulatory Commission (NRC) is currently working closely with France and Finland to ensure that the insights from the construction of a new reactor in Finland are integrated into future U.S. regulatory activities. In addition to this effort, the NRC and the Energy Department should jointly commission a detailed study on lessons learned from recent worldwide efforts to build new nuclear reactors, incorporate the commission's recommendations, and hold forums to discuss these issues with nuclear industry officials and other stakeholders.

Progress must be made toward resolving the nuclear waste problem both by individual countries and through regional compacts.

- *Finding #2*: An effective NRC is needed to ensure the safe operation of existing U.S. plants and the safe development of a new generation of U.S. plants. The NRC has good regulations to ensure the safe construction and operation of light water nuclear power plants, and its regulatory system is more open than that of other countries. Nonetheless, robust oversight is critical to the safe operation of the existing fleet and requires a strong safety culture and analytical tools. This is all the more true in light of efforts to extend the operational life of some reactors from 40 to 60 years and to increase the power output from others.

- *Recommendation #2*: The NRC should vigilantly and proactively enforce its current regulations and encourage a strong safety culture to reduce the risk of significant operating events that can lead to extensive plant shutdowns. The Energy Department, in collaboration with the NRC, should also create a new research and development program in nuclear engineering to provide the advanced tools needed to analyze the safety of reactor designs, fuels, siting options, etc. This would allow the NRC to independently analyze new reactor designs with the expectation that such an approach can lead to transparently safer and less costly projects.

- *Finding #3*: Potential bottlenecks in constructing a nuclear plant include: a) shortages of skilled trades people for plant construction and skilled personnel to design and operate plants safely and efficiently; and b) a relatively limited manufacturing base, especially for large reactor components such as heavy forgings.

- *Recommendation #3*: As part of this effort, to address labor force needs, the federal government should fund university nuclear engineering programs through the Energy Department; grants should include direct funding to support research at both the undergraduate and graduate level.

- *Finding #4*: Once U.S. utilities build a few nuclear plants, they will better understand the costs and construction times for future plants, and the market may be more favorable to building additional plants. To build the first several plants (approximately 7 to 8 reactors), industry may need more loan guarantees from the U.S. government than the roughly $18 billion that is authorized in the Energy Policy Act of 2005.

- *Recommendation #4*: The new administration should encourage public investments in low carbon-emitting electric generation alternatives, including new nuclear power plants.

- *Finding #5*: From an international perspective, two issues need to be addressed: First, progress must be made toward resolving the nuclear waste problem both by individual countries and through regional compacts. Second, the spread of nuclear power to non-nuclear weapon states will increase the likelihood of nuclear weapons proliferation from both state and non-state actors, unless governments remain vigilant and provide increased support to the International Atomic Energy Agency (IAEA).

- *Recommendation #5*: The Energy Department should fund projects that find creative solutions via regional partnerships to the nuclear waste created from reactor operation; these grants should include representatives from the countries under discussion. The United States should provide adequate funding to the IAEA to carry out necessary nonproliferation work on a growing industry. Importantly, the nuclear industry should strive to reduce the proliferation potential of its reactors and fuel cycle facilities and regularly revisit this risk.

- *Finding #6*: The safe operation of power reactors requires international safety standards that should be implemented by a suitable international institution. That institution should work to promote and ensure safe plant design and operations and develop mechanisms that could assist member countries in enforcing those standards.

- *Recommendation #6*: The United States and other nations with an interest in expanding nuclear energy should increase their funding of the IAEA and enable the agency to strengthen its existing role. The IAEA should also work with the regulatory agencies of those member countries that have extensive nuclear power programs and experience to develop global safety standards.

- *Finding #7*: The construction and operation of new power plants and fuel cycle facilities raises the risks of nuclear weapons proliferation. Given that the use of a nuclear weapon or an accidental explosion anywhere in the world might bring about a global renunciation of nuclear energy, it is in the interest of the global nuclear industry to be centrally involved in stemming weapons proliferation. Presently, security and regulatory standards differ from country to country, as do gaps in enforcement of existing standards.

- *Recommendation #7*: Develop standards for the physical protection of fissile materials to assure the physical security of civilian nuclear fuel cycle facilities and power reactors. A variety of interest groups, including regulators, the nuclear industry, experts, and nongovernmental organizations, should be consulted as part of this process.

- *Finding #8*: Nuclear weapons states (particularly the United States and Russia) must work to fulfill their nuclear disarmament commitments, with deeper reductions in their nuclear arsenals. The failure of weapons states to do so prevents overall progress on nonproliferation of nuclear technologies and weapons.

- *Recommendation #8*: Proceed with transparent, unilateral reductions in nuclear weapons, while negotiating further bilateral and multilateral reductions. The United States needs to lead the way to deeper reductions in U.S. and Russian nuclear arsenals, to be followed by multilateral reductions.

- *Finding #9*: The expansion of nuclear power could contribute further to a discriminatory and counterproductive nuclear energy regime that splits nations into two categories: those who have access to specific nuclear technologies and those who do not.

- *Recommendation #9*: A group of U.S. scientists and experts should continue working with the IAEA and ongoing international efforts to explore nondiscriminatory fuel leasing and fuel services approaches for the United States that would strengthen the Nuclear Non-Proliferation Treaty and the nonproliferation regime.

Organizations to Contact

The editors have compiled the following list of organizations concerned with the issues debated in this book. The descriptions are derived from materials provided by the organizations. All have publications or information available for interested readers. The list was compiled on the date of publication of the present volume; names, addresses, phone and fax numbers, and e-mail and Internet addresses may change. Be aware that many organizations take several weeks or longer to respond to inquiries, so allow as much time as possible.

American Nuclear Society (ANS)
555 North Kensington Avenue, La Grange Park, IL   60526
(800) 323-3044 • fax: (708) 352-0499
Web site: www.new.ans.org

The American Nuclear Society (ANS) is a nonprofit, international, scientific and educational organization that works to promote the awareness and understanding of the application of nuclear science and technology. Since its founding in 1954, ANS has developed a membership composed of approximately eleven thousand engineers, scientists, administrators, and educators representing sixteen hundred plus corporations, educational institutions, and government agencies. The ANS Web site contains a public information window that provides publications such as news briefs and position statements.

Beyond Nuclear
6930 Carroll Avenue, Suite 400, Takoma Park, MD   20912
(301) 270-2209 • fax: (301) 270-4000
e-mail: info@beyondnuclear.org
Web site: www.beyondnuclear.org

Beyond Nuclear is an advocacy organization that seeks to educate and activate the public in regards to the connections between nuclear power and nuclear weapons and the need to abandon both to safeguard our future. The Beyond Nuclear team works with diverse partners and allies to provide the public, government officials, and the media with information about the dangers of nuclear power. The group's Web site is a great source of overview information about each aspect of nuclear power as well as other publications such as fact sheets, reports, press releases, congressional testimony, articles, and videos. Recent publications include two fact sheets: *The Nuclear Power Nuclear Weapons Link* and *New Nuclear Power Plants: An NRDC Fact Sheet.*

Greenpeace International

Ottho Heldringstraat 5, The Netherlands   1066
   Amsterdam
+ 31 20 718 2000 • fax: +31 20 718 2002
e-mail: supporter.services.int@greenpeace.org
Web site: www.greenpeace.org/international/campaigns/
nuclear#

Greenpeace International is an independent global campaigning organization that acts to change attitudes and behaviors to protect and conserve the environment and to promote peace. The group's goals include promoting an energy revolution to address climate change and working for the elimination of nuclear weapons. Greenpeace is opposed to nuclear power, and a search of its Web site produces numerous reports and publications relevant to this issue. Recent publications, for example, include *The Economics of Nuclear Power* and *The Nuclear Calendar—365 Reasons to Oppose Nuclear Power.*

Nuclear Energy Institute (NEI)

1776 I Street NW, Suite 400, Washington, DC   20006-3708
(202) 739-8000 • fax: (202) 785-4019
Web site: www.nei.org

The Nuclear Energy Institute (NEI) is the policy organization of the nuclear energy and technologies industry and participates in both the national and global policy-making process. NEI's objective is to ensure the formation of policies that promote the beneficial uses of nuclear energy and technologies in the United States and around the world. The group's Web site contains a section that addresses the key issues in the nuclear power debate as well as a resources section that directs researchers to various reports, brochures, graphics, and other publications. The group also publishes a monthly newsletter, *Nuclear Energy Insight*.

Union of Concerned Scientists (UCS)

Two Brattle Square, Cambridge, MA   02238-9105
(617) 547-5552 • fax: (617) 864-9405
Web site: www.ucsusa.org/nuclear_power

The Union of Concerned Scientists (UCS) was founded in 1969 by a group of scientists and students at the Massachusetts Institute of Technology to protest the militarization of scientific research and to promote science in the public interest. Since its founding, UCS has focused on nuclear weapons and nuclear power, but it also is concerned with other issues such as global warming, clean energy, food and agriculture, and invasive species. The UCS Web site is a good source of information about nuclear power and its risks and problems. Recent UCS publications include *Nuclear Power Loan Guarantees: Another Taxpayer Bailout Ahead?* and *Nuclear Power: A Resurgence We Can't Afford*.

U.S. Department of Energy—Office of Nuclear Energy

1000 Independence Avenue SW, Washington, DC   20585
(202) 586-5000
Web site: www.ne.doe.gov

The Office of Nuclear Energy, a part of the U.S. Department of Energy, promotes nuclear power as a resource capable of meeting the nation's energy, environmental, and national security needs by resolving technical and regulatory barriers through research, development, and demonstration. The Web site contains a public information center, which provides publications, press releases, reports, congressional testimony, and other information. Other publications on the Web site include fact sheets titled *Nuclear Energy—An Overview* and *Generation IV Nuclear Energy Systems.*

U.S. Nuclear Regulatory Commission (NRC)

U.S. Nuclear Regulatory Commission
Washington, DC   20555-0001
(800) 368-5642
Web site: www.nrc.gov

The U.S. Nuclear Regulatory Commission (NRC) was created as an independent agency by Congress in 1974 to help the nation safely use radioactive materials for beneficial civilian purposes while ensuring that people and the environment are protected. The NRC regulates commercial nuclear power plants and other uses of nuclear materials, such as in nuclear medicine, through licensing, inspection, and enforcement of its requirements. The NRC's Web site provides information about the location and regulation of U.S. nuclear reactors as well as other issues such as radioactive waste disposal and nuclear security.

World Nuclear Association (WNA)

22a St James's Square, London   SW1Y 4JH
   United Kingdom
+44 (0)20 7451 1520 • fax: +44 (0)20 7839 1501
e-mail: wna@world-nuclear.org
Web site: www.world-nuclear.org

The World Nuclear Association (WNA) supports the global nuclear energy industry and promotes the use of nuclear power worldwide. The WNA Web site is a good source of information about next generation nuclear designs and also offers various publications, including position statements, speeches, and reports, such as *Ensuring Security of Supply in the International Nuclear Fuel Cycle* and *The New Economics of Nuclear Power.*

Bibliography

Books

David Bodansky   *Nuclear Energy: Principles, Practices, and Prospects*. New York: Springer, 2004.

Helen Caldicott   *Nuclear Power Is Not the Answer.* New York: New Press, 2006.

Stephanie Cooke   *In Mortal Hands: A Cautionary History of the Nuclear Age.* New York: Bloomsbury, 2009.

Gwyneth Cravens   *Power to Save the World: The Truth About Nuclear Energy.* New York: Vintage, 2008.

Pete V. Domenici, Blythe J. Lyons, and Julian J. Steyn   *A Brighter Tomorrow: Fulfilling the Promise of Nuclear Energy.* Lanham, MD: Rowman & Littlefield, 2004.

Alan M. Herbst and George W. Hopley   *Nuclear Energy Now: Why the Time Has Come for the World's Most Misunderstood Energy Source.* New York: Wiley, 2007.

Ian Hore-Lacy   *Nuclear Energy in the 21st Century.* Burlington, MA: Elsevier, 2006.

James Mahaffey   *Atomic Awakening: A New Look at the History and Future of Nuclear Power.* New York: Pegasus Books, 2009.

Arjun Makhijani   *Carbon-Free and Nuclear-Free: A Roadmap for U.S. Energy Policy.* Muskegon, MI: RDR Books, 2007.

Ewan McLeish   *The Pros and Cons of Nuclear Power.* New York: Rosen Central, 2008.

Brice Smith   *Insurmountable Risks: The Dangers of Using Nuclear Power to Combat Global Climate Change.* Muskegon, MI: RDR Books, 2006.

Galen J. Suppes and Truman Storvick, eds.   *Sustainable Nuclear Power (Sustainable World).* Boston: Academic Press, 2007.

William Tucker   *Terrestrial Energy: How Nuclear Energy Will Lead the Green Revolution and End America's Energy Odyssey.* Savage, MD: Bartleby Press, 2008.

Robert Vandenbosch and Susanne E. Vandenbosch   *Nuclear Waste Stalemate: Political and Scientific Controversies.* Salt Lake City, UT: University of Utah Press, 2007.

R. Stephen White   *Energy for the Public: The Case for Increased Nuclear Fission Energy.* California: BookSurge Pub, 2005.

Periodicals

Patricia Brett   "The Dilemma of Aging Nuclear Plants," *New York Times*, October 19, 2009. ww.nytimes.com.

Mark Clayton   "How Green Is Nuclear Power?" *Christian Science Monitor*, March 7, 2007. www.csmonitor.com.

Mark Clayton   "Nuclear Power's New Debate: Cost," *Christian Science Monitor*, August 13, 2009. www.csmonitor.com.

Steven Cohen   "Just Say No: Nuclear Power Is Complicated, Dangerous, and Definitely Not the Answer," *Grist*, August 8, 2006. www.grist.org.

Steve Connor   "Nuclear Power? Yes Please ... ," *Independent*, February 23, 2009. www.independent.co.uk.

Shikha Dalmia, William Tucker, and Jerry Taylor   "Nuclear Power and Energy Independence: A Reason Foundation Roundtable," *Reason*, October 22, 2008. http://reason.com.

Paul Davidson   "Nuclear Power Inches Back into Energy Spotlight," *USA Today*, March 30, 2009. www.usatoday.com.

Peter Fairley   "Cleaner Nuclear Power?" *Technology Review*, November 27, 2007. www.technologyreview.com.

Kent Garber   "Trying to Make Nuclear Power Less Risky," *U.S. News & World Report*, March 25, 2009. www.usnews.com.

Julio Godoy   "ENVIRONMENT: Heat Wave Shows Limits of Nuclear Energy," Inter Press Service, July 27, 2006. http://ipsnews.net.

Maya Grinberg | "Japanese Earthquake Renews Nuclear Energy Safety Concerns," *Risk Management*, September 1, 2007. www.allbusiness.com.

H. Josef Hebert | "Nuclear Energy Becomes Pivotal in Climate Debate," Associated Press, October 25, 2009.

James A. Lake, Ralph G. Bennett, and John F. Kotek | "Next Generation Nuclear Power," *Scientific American*, January 26, 2009. www.scientificamerican.com.

Marianne Lavelle | "A Worker Shortage in the Nuclear Industry," *U.S. News & World Report*, March 13, 2008. www.usnews.com.

Katherine Ling | "Nuclear Power Cannot Solve Climate Change," *Scientific American*, March 27, 2009. www.scientificamerican.com.

Scientific American | "The Future of Nuclear Power," 2009. www.scientificamerican.com.

Benjamin Sovacool | "Nuclear Power Is a False Solution to Climate Change," *Jakarta Post*, July 15, 2008. www.thejakartapost.com.

Matthew L. Wald | "Nuclear Energy: Overview," *New York Times*, October 29, 2009. www.nytimes.com.

Matthew L. Wald | "Nuclear Power May Be in Early Stages of a Revival," *New York Times*, October 23, 2008. www.nytimes.com.

Bryan Walsh | "Is Nuclear Power Viable?" *TIME*, June 6, 2008. www.time.com.

| *Wired* | "Inconvenient Truths: Get Ready to Rethink What It Means to Be Green," May 19, 2008. www.wired.com. |
| Fareed Zakaria | "A Renegade Against Greenpeace: Why He Says They're Wrong to View Nuclear Energy as 'Evil,'" *Newsweek*, April 21, 2000. www.newsweek.com. |

Index